AN INTRODUCTION TO
CHRISTIAN EDUCATION

An
Introduction To
Christian Education

By

Peter P. Person

BAKER BOOK HOUSE
Grand Rapids 6, Michigan
1961

First Printing, June 1958
Second Printing, November 1959
Third Printing, March 1961

Preface

"Of making many books there is no end," declares the author of the book of Ecclesiastes. Never was the truth of that statement more clearly demonstrated than in our twentieth century. Therefore every new book emerging from the printing press and seeking space on the already crowded library shelves must justify its very existence. Does it meet a need not otherwise adequately met?

For a number of years we have searched the book market in vain for a satisfactory textbook to use in an introductory course in Christian education on the college Freshman or Sophomore levels. Such a book should give a brief historical sketch of the movements and agencies in the field of modern Christian education. Furthermore, it should be conservative and evangelical without being antagonistic towards more liberal educational philosophies and pedagogical patterns. Denominationally it should be neutral without denying the place and purpose of denominations. It should be *interdenominational* rather than *nondenominational*.

It is in an attempt to meet this need that we have edited and elaborated the lecture notes we have used in the classroom during a number of years. The materials have been selected with the layworker and the beginning student of religious education in mind, rather than for graduate schools and advanced students. The review questions serve as a check on the students' intelligent reading of the contents of each chapter. The questions for discussion may be used for class discussion or as written assignments. Fully conscious of the limitations of such a superficial survey of Christian education, these materials have been compiled with the hope that they may inspire students to further study.

April, 1958

P. P. P.

Table of Contents

Introduction

The United States of America is historically a Christian country. It was born Christian. Other so-called Christian countries have had a pagan origin, but have adopted Christianity through the influence of missionaries. England had its Augustine, Ireland its Saint Patrick, Scotland its Columba, and the Scandinavian countries their Ansgar.

The very discovery of America reflects a Christian influence. One of the three vessels of the expedition bore a Christian name, Santa Maria (Saint Mary). To the island on which Columbus and his men landed they gave a Christian name, *San Salvador* (Holy Savior). In the opening pages of his well-kept journal Columbus states that the purpose of his venture was to discover new lands and new people *"with a view that they might be converted to our holy faith."* For his services Columbus was to receive a material reward, according to a contract drawn up April 17, 1492. Perhaps his personal motives were not altogether missionary ones. But that missionary motives were among the expressed reasons for the venture is evident from Columbus' own words.

When the sponsors of the expedition, Ferdinand and Isabella of Spain, reported the success of the venture to Pope Alexander VI, himself a Spaniard, they told of the discovery of remote islands producing gold, silver, and spices, and mentioned that the inhabitants of these islands *seemed fitted for Christianity*. The report thus conveyed the idea that the expedition had been a successful missionary as well as financial venture.

Although not all of the early settlers came to America prompted by religious motives, those who have contributed most to the founding of our nation were religious refugees. Persecuted in their home land for their unwillingness to conform to the established pattern of faith and worship, they came in search of a land where they might worship God according to the dictates of their conscience. Early colonial history records the controversies and persecution of one religious group by another, but this was evidence of Christian zeal, even though at times this zeal lacked intelligent control.

9

The church occupied a central position in the towns of early New England. The tourist traveling through modern New England is struck with the location of the old churches in the town square. Socially and educationally the church wielded a great influence. The social life of the people centered around the church. Education was sponsored by the church. The *New England Primer,* the reader used in elementary schools for more than a century, was not only religious in content; it contained elementary Christian doctrine as well.

The colonial colleges were not merely church sponsored. They were founded for the purpose of giving training to future ministers of the gospel, so that it would not become necessary *to leave an illiterate ministry to the churches, when our present ministers lie in the dust.* Thus the founders of Harvard College expressed their purposes. Yale, Brown, and other early colleges had similar ministerial objectives. Dartmouth College grew out of the effort of a clergyman, Eleazer Wheelock, to "Christianize the Indians." He was granted a charter in 1770 locating his school at Hanover, New Hampshire.

But the Christian college movement was not limited to New England. As migration moved westward, the circuit rider moved with these migrants. As the people settled here and there, chapels and churches were built and congregations were organized. The small Christian college followed. The faculty consisted largely of clergymen and returned missionaries. Many of these schools did not survive. Some of them, in spite of their ambition, never reached beyond the secondary school level but lived and died as Christian academies, even though they were adorned with the name college. With the rapid growth and expansion of state owned and supported colleges and universities, we are apt to forget the wholesome influence of these Christian colleges of the early days. From these colleges have come many of our statesmen and educators.

On April 30, 1789, George Washington was inaugurated as the first president of the United States of America. At nine o'clock that morning all the church bells of New York, the city where the inauguration was to take place, called the people together for prayer. After Washington had delivered his inaugural address, "the entire congress went on foot to St. Paul's Church where they heard prayers." Thus our nation was given a Christian birth. The presidential oath of office is still taken on the Bible, by which act we officially recognize the Bible as our highest authority.

We are grateful to God for this national Christian heritage. But we are facing a new world; we are living in a new age. We have become accustomed to the term "a Scientific Age"; we are being introduced to another, "the Atomic Age." During the first half of the twentieth century we have progressed from the oxcart to the jet-propelled plane. But how far have we been able to conserve Christian verities in this half century of speed and change? When we pause to take a spiritual and moral inventory, we discover conditions that cause us grave concern.

According to recent statistics nearly half of our present American population is not affiliated with religion in any form! We recall Abraham Lincoln's words in his "House Divided" speech. "I believe this government cannot endure permanently half slave and half free." These words were undoubtedly based on Matthew 12:25. Well may we ask, "Can our nation survive half Christian and half pagan?"

Of the religious half of our people it has been estimated that only one-tenth have an active, evangelical Christian faith. The low average in church attendance of members of Protestant churches is a matter of growing concern. Observing the number enrolled with the number in attendance in our Sunday schools gives us further evidence that America is no longer taking its Christianity seriously. It is not the names on the roster but the pupils actually in the church classrooms that constitute Christian education.

Those who actually attend Sunday school are often taught by untrained, poorly qualified teachers. The actual teaching time is on the average less than half an hour. Add to this the fact that in many situations you find a number of classes crowded into one large room (the church sanctuary), with a lack of blackboards and maps, and pews built for adults in place of comfortable seats for children. The problem then becomes acute. The old query, When is a school not a school? and the answer, "When it is a Sunday school," has a sharp cutting edge.

It is not how many attend regularly that is most important, but what happens to them when they are in class. Merely keeping a group of growing children within the walls of the church for an hour on Sunday may not have too much significance. In some Sunday school classes the children actually develop an attitude of irreverence for the house of God. Much of that which is called Christian education is neither Christian nor education.

Juvenile delinquency is a moral threat to our nation. Recently a government official in a lecture to educators made the statement that it has been estimated that during the current year a million of our American youth will be guilty of some form of juvenile delinquency. Sociologists, psychologists, clergymen, teachers, and judges of Juvenile Courts are agreed that the young offenders are not altogether to blame; it is the home that must bear much of the guilt. Parents are too busy making money to find time to make good homes. Religious education in the home, with its traditional daily family prayers, is often neglected, if not altogether unknown. Our American children are permitted to grow up as pagans in a so-called Christian country.

The present president of Harvard University, while president of Lawrence College, gave a clear expression of what, in his opinion, was the basic cause for our national moral decline. Said he:

"During the years just prior to the war there was a great deal of ill-founded talk about *isms* on campuses, but rarely was mention made of two *isms* which might with most reason have then been held up as reproaches to our institutions of higher learning. The first of these was simple hedonism, that way of life wherein the students lived primarily for pleasure and enjoyment in carefree irresponsibility and on some campuses, though happily not on ours, at a surprising level of ultrasophistication. The other related *ism* was and is a more serious problem, a far more widespread and a more deeply involved one. I refer to the secularism that has been characteristic of our whole society, as well as of the colleges, for a long time."[1]

It is not alone the presence of these two "isms," but the absence of a clear-cut Christian philosophy of life that has weakened the moral fiber of our nation. But the college campus is not the only area where such "isms" have wielded their subtle influence. They have penetrated into all strata of society, even into the Christian church. We adjust our way of life to that of the world at large. We have become social chameleons. As professing Christians we have ignored the Apostle Paul's warning that we "be not fashioned according to this world: but be ye transformed" (Rom. 12:2, ARV). We seem to have forgotten the prayer of Jesus for his disciples that they might be kept *in the world,* yet apart from it (John 17:15). No longer do we deserve bearing the name "Protestant," for we rarely protest against evil. Like Lot, we are vexed with the wickedness we hear and see, yet we do nothing about it (II Peter 2:8).

History repeats itself. In the history of Israel we find a sad example of neglected religious education. Moses had given a definite command to parents that they should teach their children (Deut. 6:1–9). But when Joshua, Moses' successor, died, the book of Judges

---

[1] From a semi-annual report of November 16, 1945, by Nathan Marsh Pusey, then President of Lawrence College.

records these sad words, "There arose another generation after them, that knew not Jehovah, nor yet the work which he had wrought for Israel" (Judg. 2:10). The older generation had spent its time and energy in taking material possession of the land God had given them, but at the expense of neglecting the religious education of its own children. The consequence was the dark age of the Judges. After a sordid catalogue of crimes and bloodshed the author of Judges concludes his book with an enlightening comment: "In those days there was no king in Israel; every man did that which was right in his own eyes" (Judg. 21:25). There was moral as well as political confusion.

But Hebrew history also records religious revivals brought about through a revived teaching ministry. These revivals were felt throughout the nation. In the reign of King Josiah there was one such revival (II Kings 22:8–13); during the time of Ezra there was another (Neh. 8:1–18). Church history is replete with instances where the discovery, study, and application of the sacred Scriptures have brought about spiritual awakenings. We sometimes quote the saying, "Whatever man has done, man may do." It is also true that: "Whatever God has done (in the past), God may do (now and in the future)."

It is with this in mind, America's spiritual and moral needs, and God's saving grace and power, that we focus our attention upon the Christian church and its teaching ministry. If the Christian church is to expand numerically, we must evangelize; if our individual Christians are to develop spiritually healthy lives, we must inform and edify; if our Christian America is to survive, we must recapture its early Christian spirit in order to develop a Christ-consciousness rather than our present wealth-awareness and self-consciousness.

To workers in the field of conservative Christian education the words of Mordecai to Queen Esther may well apply: "And who knoweth whether thou art not come to the kingdom for such a time as this?" (Esther 4:14).

Historical Background

STUDY OUTLINE

I. **What Is Christian Education?**
1. Religious education
2. Christian education
II. **Religious Education among Primitive People**
1. All primitive education is religious in nature
2. By nature primitive people are religious
3. They need Christian education
III. **Religious Education among Ancient Non-Christian Civilization**
1. The Chinese
   a. Confucius, Lao-tse, the classics
   b. Ethical, rather than religious education
   c. Conserve the past
2. The Hindus
   a. Aryans
   b. Caste system
   c. The Vedas
   d. Guatama and Ghandi
3. The Persians
   a. Aryans
   b. Zoroaster

c. Zend-Avesta
d. Goal: the good soldier
IV. **Religious Education among the Hebrews**
1. Origin
2. Education
   a. Family
   b. Feasts
   c. Synagogues
   d. Teachers
3. Jewish education today
V. **Christian Religious Education**
1. Early Christian schools
2. Christ, the founder
3. New people and new problems
4. Catechumenal schools
5. Catechetical schools
6. Cathedral schools
7. Protestant Reformation and education
8. Modern movements
   a. Sunday church schools
   b. Vacation church schools
   c. Weekday church schools

I. *Definition.*

Christian education is a term that denotes a relationship with general education. It is education of a particular type. *Religious education* has traditionally referred to the teaching ministry of the Christian church. Theological seminaries and Christian colleges have offered courses in *religious education.* A number of books have included the term in their titles. Thomas Nelson and Sons published a book in 1940 entitled *A Survey of Religious Education.* J. M. Price of Southwestern Baptist Theological Seminary, James

H. Chapman of Howard College, A. E. Tibbs of the Baptist Bible
Institute, and L. L. Carpenter of Baylor University collaborated
in its preparation. Except for one chapter on education among the
Jews the book deals with *Christian* education. Abingdon-Cokesbury
Press in 1950 published a large volume entitled *Orientation in
Religious Education*. The book was edited by Philip Henry Lotz.
More than two-score writers contributed articles for the book. One
of these was a Jew writing about Jewish education in America.
Another contributor was a Roman Catholic who wrote about the
program of religious education sponsored by his church.

Recently there has developed a trend in the direction of the use
of the more exclusive term *Christian* education. *Religious* education is so general as to include practically all religions that are
propagated through instruction. Two books have been published
recently that have a definite emphasis on the word *Christian* in their
titles. They are *The Church and Christian Education*, Bethany
Press (1947), and *Christian Education in a Democracy*, Oxford
Press (1951). The former, edited by Paul H. Vieth of Yale, is the
report of a committee appointed by the International Council of
Religious Education in 1944. The latter, edited by Frank E.
Gaebelein of Stony Brook School (N.Y.), is the report of a similar
committee appointed by the National Association of Evangelicals
in 1946. Both of these committees working independently of one
another have, nevertheless, arrived at similar conclusions in certain areas, while differing greatly in others. A well-informed leader
in Christian education should carefully study both of these docu-
ments.

Our intention in this study is to focus upon the teaching ministry of the Christian church rather than to attempt to explore the
wider field of religious education. We shall limit the term Christian education so as to mean *Protestant* Christian education, particularly the *Evangelical* Protestant. The author has a definite
denominational affiliation, but in directing the thinking in this
course he will strive as far as possible to be objective and to present the subject matter from an evangelical, interdenominational
point of view.

Walter Athearn has defined religious education as "the introduction of control into experience in terms of religious ideas and
ideals."[1] This definition is broad enough to include Jewish, Moham-
medan, Hindu, and all other non-Christian religions, as well as
the Christian.

---

[1] *The Minister and the Teacher*, p. 17.

Christian education has been defined by Paul H. Vieth as "the process by which persons are confronted with and controlled by the Christian gospel."[2] This definition is gospel centered. It is also Christ centered, for Christ is the heart of the gospel. It is *character* education in the sense that it modifies human nature. This change is brought about not through the imitation of an ideal personality, Jesus of Nazareth, but by means of the motivating experience of thinking and living controlled by the living Son of God, Christ our Savior. We need more than an example to live by. We need a Savior from sin, and a master of our individual lives, a dynamic.

Although our primary purpose in this study is to focus our thinking on the teaching ministry of the church, thus Christian education, a brief survey of religious education among ancient people, both primitive and civilized, will help us to appreciate the characteristics of modern evangelical Christian education. Even primitive people have developed a type of education that is basically religious.

From the time of the great missionary, Robert Morrison, until recent times, Christian nations have been sending their missionaries to China to bring the gospel message. We have called the Chinese a heathen people, even though they had a civilization long before the Christian era.

India, too, is a non-Christian country with a deeply rooted civilization. Its pattern of religious education differs greatly from our modern Christian educational organizations and techniques, but it has, nevertheless, proved very effective. The Christian missionary motivated by a burning zeal but sadly lacking in philosophical training is no match for a Brahman with his mystical philosophy. If he is to be successful in his missionary work with the educated classes of India, the missionary must possess knowledge as well as zeal.

The Persians, too, developed an effective educational system. Their sacred writings, the Zend-Avesta, were to them what our Holy Bible is to us as Christians. There is much that we may learn from the educational practices, and certainly from the zeal, of these non-Christian people. In one of his parables Jesus commended an unrighteous steward because he acted *wisely*, not righteously, saying *"the sons of this world are for their own generation wiser than the sons of light"* (Luke 16:8, ARV).

We should train ourselves to appreciate the good even when found outside of the Christian church, for God is the author of all

---

[2] *The Church and Christian Education*, p. 52.

good (Jas. 1:17), and also to detect that which is not good even when found within *the practices of the church.*
II. *Religious Education among Primitive People.*

Robert Ulich of Harvard quotes Plato's definition of education as "the process of drawing and guiding children towards that principle which is pronounced right by the law and confirmed as truly right by the experience of the oldest and most just."[3]

Although we find no formal education among primitive men, there are traditions and taboos that control their behavior. According to Plato's definition, primitive man does administer education. There are taboos that have become governing laws, not because tribal assemblies have voted them so, but because of the cumulative experiences of past generations, the experience of the "oldest and most just."

To primitive man there is no separation of life into the sacred and the secular. All of his education is religious in nature. There are deeply rooted fears of the elements of nature, of wild beasts, of enemy tribes, of evil spirits. Before the hunt or before battle he implores divine aid from his gods. His religion is largely that of animism. The great spirit to him is usually a terrifying being to be bribed or placated. Children are taught in their families the taboos and traditions of the tribe. Medicine men and priests play an important part in preserving and transmitting these sacred customs, traditions, and tribal history. Since primitive man neither writes books nor is able to read books even if he had them, he preserves the tribal history in the form of the tribal dance which is dramatized and acted out. Even his religion is expressed in pageantry. Modern missionaries ministering to pagan people record and report personal observation of the superstitions, beliefs, and practices still current among these people. The missionaries' goal is not to make the native religious, for that he is already, but to make him Christian. The primary method used by modern missionaries is an elementary type of *Christian* education. The testimony of most missionaries is that the pagan adult converted to Christianity retains much of his superstitions and fears. His soul is saved, but his thought pattern remains pagan. It is to the mission schools that minister to childhood and youth that one must look for converts with a Christian philosophy of life. It is in the second generation that the ripe fruit of Christianity is harvested.
III. *Religious Education among Ancient Non-Christian Civilizations.*

---

[3] *History of Educational Thought,* p. 6.

Asia is a large continent inhabited by a variety of people differing in patterns of thought, religion, and levels of culture. Some of these peoples represent civilizations much older than ours. They are therefore not to be classified with primitive people even though they are non-Christian.

1. *The Chinese.* Before Christ was born, the Chinese had already developed a civilization. Hence Christian missionaries who have gone to China have found a situation quite different from that of the missionaries who have gone to some of the primitive tribes in the interior of Africa.

Confucius, who lived in the sixth century before Christ, left an indelible impression upon the thought and educational patterns of China. Following the general teaching techniques of Socrates and making much use of the teachings of his contemporary Lao-tse, Confucius became the great scholar and sage of ancient China. His teachings were moral rather than religious. They dealt with duty and conduct in this present life without reference to preparation for a life beyond. Much of them dealt with conduct within the family. It was character education rather than religious education. No less than nine Chinese books are accredited to Confucius, five of which are known as the classics. They deal with political and ethical problems.

An elaborate system of examinations was developed in the Chinese educational system. In order to secure a government position it was necessary to pass this examination, which consisted almost exclusively of the ability to repeat verbatim the contents of the classics. It was an effective way of preserving the past, but contributed nothing to developing an adjustment to the future. Elmer Harrison Wilds in his book *The Foundations of Modern Education* says of them, "The highest ambition of the Chinese has been to remain as they are and to preserve the past."[4] This attitude made the work of the early Christian educational missionary most difficult. Unlike the Athenians, who were constantly seeking something new (Acts 17:21), the Chinese feared the new.

2. *The Hindus.* The peninsula of India was settled about the time of Abraham by an Aryan race related to the modern Europeans. Adolf Hitler, we remember, was seeking for a pure Aryan race from which he hoped to develop supermen. Very early in their history these Aryans became class conscious and developed a caste system. There were four recognized castes besides the *outcasts,* who were the lowest in the social level. The top stratum consisted of the

---

[4] p. 39.

Brahmans, which included the priests, teachers, and rulers. Then came the second level, the soldiers; the third caste was represented by the artisans, merchants, and money lenders; the fourth group was made up of the menials and serfs. At the very bottom of this social pyramid were the masses, the outcasts, the *untouchables*.

Hindu education was definitely religious. Unlike the teachings of Confucius, the Hindu education prepared for a life to come rather than for the present life. Among the upper classes religion was a philosophy of mysticism; among the lower classes it was superstition in its crudest form. Education was only for the priests, teachers, and rulers, thus 95 per cent of the population was deprived of educational opportunities except on a very elementary level.

The sacred books, the *Vedas*, were written in Sanskrit. Education consisted largely in the memorization of the contents of these books. The priests were given intensive training over a period of twelve years. It was from this class-conscious people that Gautama (the Buddha) and Mahatma Ghandi have come. The latter's philosophy of peaceful conquest through nonresistance has greatly influenced the history of modern India.

The Christian missionary going to the land of the Hindus to present the gospel of Christ must decide whether he will work among the upper castes or the outcasts. A missionary living among the low castes would wield no influence upon the intellectuals but would himself be considered an outcast. There is a fertile field for educational missions among the millions in India. When enlightened, the lower classes are receptive to the Christian gospel. The Brahman (a member of the highest caste) has a mind so steeped in mystical philosophy that it is extremely difficult to reach him with the gospel of Christ; difficult but not impossible.

3. *The Persians.* The Persians were a branch of the Aryan race which migrated westward towards the Caspian Sea into an area known as *Iran,* later called Persia. They were a military people. Zoroaster, their great religious leader, who lived about the time of the Jews' return to Palestine from the Babylonian captivity, was a great military leader. It was his religious military teachings that motivated the vast armies of the Medo-Persian empire. Many of his religious ideas resembled those of the Hebrew people, a personal God, a personal devil, heaven, hell, and a final day of judgment.

The primary objective of this Persian education was to produce the good soldier. The state provided military education. For their priests, the magi, there was special training in astrology, divination, medicine, and law. The "wise men" who came to pay homage to the Christ child are called magi (Matt. 2:1). In the book of Daniel we find reference to "the law of the Medes and Persians" (Dan. 6:8), understood to be rigid, unchangeable laws.

The doctrines of the Persians were preserved in their sacred literature, the *Zend-Avesta* (the Bible of the Parsees). This included laws, narratives, litanies for rituals, and hymns. After instruction in the home by the mother, the boy at seven years of age began his formal education, consisting largely of military training.

In all three of these cultures, which we have hastily surveyed, we find an emphasis on preserving the traditions and philosophies of the past. This is accomplished through memorization of the contents of the classical writings. At best education is for the upper classes and not for the masses. When we come to consider our present-day Christian education, we shall appreciate the contrasts. There was, however, one race among the many Asiatic people that rose far above its neighbors in the program of religious education it provided — the Hebrew people. Since Christianity has a direct relationship with Judaism, we shall consider religious education of Old Testament times as an introduction to our study of Christian education.

IV. *Among the Hebrews.*

The Hebrew people do not emerge in history as savages. Abraham, the father of the Hebrew race, came from Ur of the Chaldees in Mesopotamia. This land *between the rivers* (Tigris and Euphrates) was a fertile delta, whose people early in world history developed a civilization. Excavations by archeologists at Ur have brought to light a wealth of cultural evidence in the form of inscribed clay tablets which scholars have deciphered. The Code of Hammurabi reflects a consciousness of moral, social, and economic problems. Hammurabi lived about 2200-2000 B.C., thus about the time of Abraham.

The patriarchs, Abraham, Isaac, and Jacob, owned large herds and flocks, which necessitated a nomadic type of life. But being nomadic does not preclude culture. The book of Genesis provides a wealth of source materials for a study of the social and cultural life of that period.

During their long stay in Egypt the families of the sons of Jacob developed into independent tribes. They preserved their culture in the midst of the Egyptian environment. The presence of an alien group that refused to become assimilated into the Egyptian culture caused the new Egyptian dynasty considerable concern (Exod. 1:8-10). The pharaoh of an earlier dynasty had permitted them to

settle in "the best of the land" (Gen. 47:6). For the safety of the
new dynasty these aliens must be subjected to control.

The bondage inflicted upon them by the new dynasty failed to
crush these aliens. They continued their own social customs and
methods of religious worship. The common misery only tended
to bring these twelve tribal families closer together. Moses, the
self-exiled Egyptian prince of Hebrew birth and Egyptian education, united the tribes into a federation which might well have been
called *The United Tribes of Israel.* At Mount Sinai the Ten Commandments were given; rules regulating personal conduct as well
as formal religious worship were formulated. The Tribe of Levi
was set apart as priests. A portable temple, the tabernacle (a tent),
was prescribed and prepared.

Since the Hebrews were a devout religious people, their education
was religious in nature. The family was the educational unit, with
the parents as the teachers. Moses gave an educational mandate
charging the parents with the religious instruction of their own
children, "when thou sittest in thy house, and when thou walkest
by the way, and when thou liest down, and when thou risest up"
(Deut. 6:7). It was not mere ten-minute family prayers, but continuous instruction from early morning until late at night. It was
at home religious instruction.

The family feasts were religious in nature and were dramatized
in such a way that even the children could participate. The weekly
Sabbath was introduced by the lighting of the candles. Even small
children are interested in candles.

Each year the Passover Feast with its ritual reviewed the history
of the exodus from Egypt. The Feast of the Tabernacles with its
week of camping recalled the wilderness wanderings. The Day of
Atonement with its elaborate rituals could not have failed to impress children as well as adults. The new year was introduced
with the blowing of the trumpets. What boy is not thrilled by the
sound of wind instruments? During the wilderness wanderings the
tabernacle represented the presence of God. When the Israelites
pitched their tents, God's tent, the tabernacle, was pitched in the
midst of the camp. It impressed young and old alike with the idea
of the presence of God in their very midst.

When the Israelites entered the promised land, Canaan, they
became so occupied with taking possession of this gift of God that
they neglected to instruct their children. After Joshua, Moses' successor and the conqueror of Canaan, was dead and buried, there
arose another generation that did not know God. They had not
been given adequate religious instruction. The result was political

and religious confusion, when every man did as he pleased. The book of Judges is a sad but graphic commentary on what happens when a nation becomes more concerned with material wealth than with religious instruction.

Out of this confused period of the judges there emerges the monarchy. Samuel, the seer, gave direction to the early years of the kingdom. There does not seem to have been any definite pattern of religious education. Jehoshaphat, the reformer-king of Judah, selected Levites and sent them throughout his kingdom to teach his subjects from the law of the Lord (II Chron. 17:7–9). In the days of Nehemiah, Ezra the scribe, with the assistance of thirteen Levites, conducted a religious school in Jerusalem (Neh. 8:1–18).

The origin of the synagogue is somewhat obscure. It developed during the period of the Babylonian captivity and was a place of instruction as well as of worship. Daily classes were conducted for children; on the Sabbath and on market days special services for adults were held. There developed a class of religious leaders, the scribes, who not only copied the Scriptures as the name implies, but they were interpreters and teachers as well. The synagogues were erected in all communities where Jews resided. A Jew was forbidden to live where there was no synagogue. There was one central temple of the Jewish faith in Jerusalem, but there were, it has been claimed, more than four hundred synagogues in Jerusalem alone.[5]

In these synagogues the Jewish elementary school developed. It provided for the instruction of boys between the ages of six and sixteen. The teachers were usually the scribes. No teacher was to have more than twenty-five pupils. If there were more he was to have an assistant. When as many as fifty were enrolled, a second teacher must be secured. These teachers served without pay, earning their living through other means. Although reading, writing, and arithmetic were included in the curriculum, the main objective was to become familiar with the Sacred Scriptures. Large sections of these Scriptures were memorized. The book of Leviticus was used in the selection of passages for memorization even by small children. The Talmud declares: "The world continues to exist only by the breath of the children of the schools."[6]

The Jew in America sends his children to the public school. The

---

[5] See J. M. Price, *A Survey of Religious Education*, p. 32.
[6] The Talmud is a body of Jewish civil and canonical laws not included in their Sacred Scriptures.

religious instruction is given in Sunday schools and on weekdays in Hebrew schools conducted after public school hours, five, four, or three times a week. In the area of modern Jewish education there are four groups: the Orthodox, the Conservative, the Reform, and the Laborites (Yiddishists).

V. *Christian Religious Education.*

1. *Early Christian schools.* Christianity has its historical roots so deeply imbedded in Hebrew history and tradition that we seem justified in referring to this relationship as Hebrew-Christian. The founder of Christianity, Jesus of Nazareth, was a member of the Hebrew race. The gospels have recorded his genealogy (Matt. 1:1-16; Luke 3:23-38). His twelve apostles were Hebrews. Paul, the apostle to the gentiles, calls himself a "Hebrew of the Hebrews" (Phil. 3:5). The first Christians were Jewish Christians who supplemented their Judaism with their acknowledgment of Jesus as their Messiah and Lord. It was the Apostle Paul who formulated in his epistles the basic principles of the Christian faith. Paul had been trained in the famous school of Gamaliel to become a rabbi. This mental discipline of the mind enabled him to crystallize the theology of the early church.

2. *Christ, the founder.* In Christ's educational program there were neither classrooms nor class schedules. The class did not meet in the Jerusalem temple nor in the Capernaum synagogue at a specified hour. It did not even have a formal curriculum. It was education through apprenticeship. For three years the pupils lived with their Teacher. They heard Him as He taught the multitudes; they watched Him as He healed individuals. They shared with Him not only at meal time, but in the periods of prayer as well. They were sent out by twos, as teaching cadets, to say what they had heard their Teacher say, and to do what they had seen Him do. The disciples had in their homes and synagogue schools become acquainted with Hebrew history; they had memorized large portions of the Scriptures. But Jesus gave new interpretations to old texts, saying, "Ye have heard that it was said . . . but I say unto you (Matt. 5:21, 22).

The rabbis of Jesus' day quoted authorities on the Jewish law. Often it was a matter of interpreting interpretations, but Jesus spoke with authority without resorting to the quoting of rabbinical authorities. The comment about the multitudes after they heard Jesus preach what we commonly call The Sermon on the Mount is significant: "The multitudes were astonished at his teaching: for he taught them as one having authority, and not as their scribes" (Matt. 7:28, 29). The officers who were sent by the chief priests and Pharisees to arrest Jesus returned empty handed; when asked "Why did ye not bring him?" their answer was brief but pertinent, "Never man so spake" (John 7:45, 46).

3. *New people and new problems.* As long as the disciples ministered to Jerusalem Jews, there was no need for independent schools. The Sacred Scriptures were taught in the synagogue schools. The Messianic hope was prominent in Judaism. The disciples could build their teaching on this Jewish foundation by pronouncing that the crucified and resurrected Jesus was the Messiah.

When the gospel message was extended to non-Jewish people the situation changed. These gentiles were not familiar with the Hebrew Scriptures and the traditions of Judaism. It became necessary to give them background. The Old Testament, which had been translated into Greek in the third century before Christ, became an agent in this new missionary venture, for Greek was the language of most people of the Roman empire. Since civil law and government was dominated by the Romans, it was but natural that later education would take on a Roman pattern.

4. *Catechumenal schools.* Before these gentile converts could be admitted into the fellowship of the church, they needed to be instructed in the basic teachings of the church. So-called catechumenal schools were established to give this instruction. There were three grades or classes. The first or lowest grade was the *hearers.* They listened to the reading of the Scriptures and to sermons. The second grade was that of *kneelers.* These remained for prayers. They knelt. The third and last grade was that of the *chosen.* These were the candidates for baptism. If the proper progress was not in evidence, the convert could be retarded in his class, demoted or rejected. This probation before admittance into the fellowship of the church extended over a period of two or three years. Later the course was enriched and extended to four years for the children of Christians. Girls as well as boys were admitted. At first able members of the church served as teachers. Later deacons and special teachers were responsible for the instruction.

5. *Catechetical schools.* The catechumenal schools were elementary and served merely to prepare candidates for membership in the church. When philosophers and other educated persons became converts to Christianity, it became necessary to establish Christian schools of higher education. Pantaenus, a converted Stoic philosopher, became head of such a school at Alexandria in Egypt. His aim was to reconcile Christianity with Greek philosophy, thus to present Christianity as academically respectable. Other similar schools came into being. They served to train church leaders.

The content of the studies was philosophical rather than biblical.

6. *Cathedral schools.* As Christianity spread through the Roman empire, bishoprics were established. In each bishopric theological schools were founded for the training of the clergy. These schools were held in the Cathedrals, hence the name *Cathedral schools.* These gradually took the place of the Catechetical schools.

7. *The Protestant Reformation and education.* During the Dark Ages, when paganism cast its shadows over the entire civilized world, it was the church that kept the candle of culture burning in an otherwise dark world. With the Renaissance a new era began. A part of this awakening was the Protestant Reformation. Martin Luther's insistence on the shift of authority from the word of church councils to that of the Word of God as revealed in the Bible, brought about a radical change in education. If the public was to refer to the Bible as its authority, each individual had to be able to read the Bible. The Bible was originally written in Hebrew, Aramaic, and Greek. It had been translated into Greek (Septuagint) and Latin (Vulgate), but only the scholars read Greek and Latin. Luther then proceeded to translate the Bible into German. But not all Germans could read. This made it necessary to establish public schools so that the German children could learn to read, in order that they might read and understand the Bible, in order that they might be saved. The German public schools (Volkschule) had a definite Christian objective.

The Catholic Church also experienced a reformation, sometimes referred to as the Counter Reformation. The teaching ministry was stressed. Ignatius Loyola, a Spanish nobleman, founded the Society of Jesus, more generally known as Jesuits. It is even today one of the strong teaching-orders of the Catholic Church. Its motto was "All for the greater glory of God"; its aim, "a Christian gentleman and a Christian scholar." The Protestant aim was to develop a religious and moral life in the individual through his own interpretation of the Bible. The Catholic aim *was to subject the individual to institutional control.* The Protestants aimed to reach all ages and classes; the Jesuits aimed at training leaders. The Jesuits were organized along military lines; all members were responsible to their General, and he, in turn, to the Pope. They have been referred to as the Catholic Salvation Army. The method consisted of memory drills with frequent reviews. To maintain interest there were prizes, ranks, and rivalry. Each boy vied with a rival. The candidates were carefully selected and then subjected to an intensive training. This training was continued until the candidate was past twenty years of age, when he became a teacher. He might

then be selected for advanced training at some Jesuit University.
Although the aim of Protestant education was the saving of the
soul, it was not limited to that. Luther at one time expressed himself as follows: "Were there neither soul, heaven, nor hell, it would
still be necessary to have schools for the sake of affairs here below."
He went on to say: "The world has need of educated men and
women to the end that men may govern the country properly and
women may properly bring up their children, care for the domestics,
and direct the affairs of their households."

8. *Modern movements.* A number of movements have come into
being during the past two centuries. The most notable are those
of the *Sunday church school* (1785), The *vacation church school*
(1901), and the *weekday church school* (1914). These and other
organizations for the promotion of Christian education will be
considered in later chapters.

From the preceding historical survey we note that religious education is not a new movement. It is as old as the human race. The
patterns may vary with the different races and geographical loca-
tions, but the objective is the same — to develop a religious life.
Christian education, though a type of religious education, is more
sharply defined. It is Christ-centered. Its goal is to produce the
Christian. The methods and materials may vary as we shall learn
later, but unless it has Christ at its core, it is not worthy of the
name *Christian Education.*

REVIEW QUESTIONS

1. What is the difference between *religious* education and *Christian* education?
2. Who are the teachers among primitive people?
3. What is the content of their teaching?
4. Why do we not classify the Chinese as primitive people?
5. Who was Confucius?
6. In what sense are his teachings not religious?
7. Describe the caste system of the Hindus.
8. What constituted their sacred scriptures?
9. Name two of its leaders, one ancient, one modern.
10. Where do the Persians contact Hebrew history?
11. Who was their great military leader?
12. What constituted their sacred scriptures?
13. In what language were they written?
14. Where was the childhood home of Abraham?
15. May a nomad be a person of culture? Explain.
16. What was the original unit of Hebrew education?

17. How did the Hebrew festivals contribute to religious education?
18. What was the synagogue?
19. Who were the teachers in ancient Israel?
20. What is the nature of Hebrew education in America today?
21. What religious background did the first Christians have?
22. What change in the members of the church made an educational change necessary?
23. What contribution did Luther make to education?
24. Who were the Jesuits?
25. Name three modern movements in Christian education.

QUESTIONS FOR DISCUSSION

1. Do leaders in Christian education need to be familiar with the religious education plans and programs of non-Christian groups? Give reasons for your answer.
2. In what ways may zealous missionaries without a cultural background offend the cultured Chinese?
3. Why is it so difficult to convert the Hindu to Christianity?
4. Should a Christian missionary strive to convert the upper classes or the outcasts? Give reasons for your answer.
5. Why is missionary work among the modern Jews so difficult?
6. Explain: "Hebrew is to the modern Jewish child a foreign language."
7. To what extent were the early Christian schools influenced by Hebrew patterns of education? Greek? Roman?
8. In what way was the Protestant Reformation of benefit to the Roman Catholic Church?
9. What are the advantages and disadvantages of a regimented system of education, such as that of the Jesuits?
10. How does church history contribute to the understanding of modern Christian education?

2

The Christian Church

STUDY OUTLINE

The Apostle's Creed is a brief summary of the religious belief of Christians in general. There are different interpretations of the terms within the creed as well as different versions of the creed. Most Christians, however, would accept it as the approximation of their personal religious beliefs.

But a creed is a mere parade of vocabulary unless the words convey a definite meaning. As a part of our childhood religious instruction we memorized the Ten Commandments, the Lord's Prayer, and the Apostles' Creed, besides many Bible passages. This was accomplished through rote memory by means of drill. We often mechanically recite these words we have memorized, without awareness of what we are saying. It is possible to *pray* the so-called Lord's Prayer, but most often we *recite* it in parrot-like fashion.

When we recite the Apostles' Creed we solemnly affirm that "I believe in the holy Christian Church."[1] It is a personal testimony: "I believe." But what do we believe about the church? Much of the criticism that has been directed against the Christian church during our generation has been by individuals who have failed to understand the basic nature and function of the church. An introduction to a study of Christian education must begin with a consideration of the church itself.

I. *Definitions.*

In modern usage our English term *church* is used in a variety of ways, four in particular. In the gospels the term occurs only twice, both times in Matthew (16:18; 18:17). The first refers to the words of Jesus to Peter, "Upon this rock I will build my church." The second instance deals with church discipline and the sinning brother, "Tell it unto the church, and if he refuse to hear the church also, let him be unto thee as the Gentile and the publican."

It is the book of Acts that introduces the Christian church as a body of active believers in Christ. The epistles discuss the nature and function of the church. They are concerned with correcting errors in the believer's thinking and inconsistencies in his conduct. (II Tim. 4:1-4; II Cor. 6:14-16). The Book of Revelation directs its messages through "the seven churches that are in Asia" to all churches of all time (Rev. 1:4).

1. *The church as a building.* In popular usage a church is a structure where Christian worship is conducted. Newspapers report that a certain church has burned or that a congregation plans to build a new church. The slogan "Go to church Sunday" is based upon this use of the word. It literally means that one should on Sunday go to some building where religious services are conducted.

2. *The church as a local congregation.* A group of Christian believers banded together by a common faith into a congregation is also referred to as a church. The local church in a community is usually identified through the location of its place of worship, *Belden Avenue* Baptist Church; or its founder, *Moody* Memorial Church; or by some biblical name, *Bethany* Methodist Church. Except for nondenominational congregations such as Community Churches or Bible Churches, the denominational designation is usually included in the corporate name, Saint Peter's *Episcopal* Church. Sometimes when there are several churches of the same denomina-

---

[1] Some versions render it as holy Catholic Church, *Catholic* meaning universal.

tion in the same city, they are referred to by chronological order,
The *Fourth* Presbyterian Church.

3. *The church as a denomination.* A denomination is an organization of individual congregations united through common doctrinal views and administrative practices. The term "church" is usually included in the corporate name of denominations, as in The *Presbyterian* Church U.S.A.

4. *The universal church.* Theologically the Christian Church is the sum total of all believers in Christ irrespective of denominational or local congregational affiliation. The Apostle Paul refers to both the local church and the collective, or universal Church. He addresses two of his epistles to "the church of God which is at Corinth" (I Cor. 1:2; II Cor. 1:1). Likewise he addresses two epistles to "the church of the Thessalonians" (I Thess. 1:1; II Thess. 1:1). In his epistles to the Ephesians and the Colossians he uses the term church in a more inclusive sense, meaning all believers in Christ (Eph. 5:27; Col. 1:18). Paul uses the analogy of the human body, Christ is the head while the church is the body. The wishes of the head are carried out through the members of the body.

Georgia Harkness, in her book *Understanding the Christian Faith,* presents a concise definition of the church — "The Christian church is a fellowship of persons united by a common loyalty to Christ and by a desire to worship and do the will of God as revealed in Christ."[2] Note that it is a fellowship rather than a membership, an organism rather than an organization. The spiritual life thus becomes of primary importance; the organization, though necessary, becomes secondary. The common loyalty to Christ means discipleship. It was loyalty to their Master that kept the group of disciples intact. "When this central loyalty to Christ is lost, as sometimes happens, the church is no longer a church but a secular club not very different from any other group."[3]

In our study of the teaching ministry of the church we shall focus our thinking largely on the local church. Denominational headquarters may give directives and offer suggestions, but it is in the local church that Christian education functions. The teaching ministry of a denomination will be no better than the work in the local churches.

II. *The Origin of the Christian Church.*

In order to understand the purpose and function of any institution or organization, it is essential to trace its historical roots.

---

[2] p. 149.
[3] *Ibid.,* p. 150.

The Christian church as an institution has deep roots extending beyond the realms of time to the original idea in the mind of God.

1. *The church originated in the mind of God.* The history of the Christian church is so vitally related to the divine plan of human redemption as to be inseparable. Theologically the Church originated in the mind of God before the foundation of the world was laid. So declare both Paul and Peter (Eph. 3:9–11; I Pet. 1:20). Long before sin entered the human race, God had formulated a plan of salvation. Sin did not come as a surprise to God. He had anticipated it and provided for it. Christ was to become God incarnate; He was to be born as a human, son of man as well as Son of God. He was to be the Lamb of God that taketh away the sin of the world (John 1:29). He was to die on the cross of Calvary, to be raised from the dead on the third day, and ascend into heaven, leaving his disciples on earth as his body — the Head in heaven, the body on earth, the latter carrying out the will of the former. The Holy Spirit operates through the members of the Christian Church. Note such passages as Acts 13:2, and Colossians 3:1–4 and 2:19. The Holy Spirit came to earth as Christ's successor (John 14:26; 16:7, 14). It was all planned from eternity.

2. *Historically the church was born at Pentecost.* When Jesus ascended to heaven, he gave to his disciples what we have come to call the *missionary mandate* (Matt. 28:19, 20). They were commanded to go forth making disciples in the Name of the triune God — Father, Son, and Holy Spirit. But they were also instructed to wait for the coming of the Holy Spirit (Acts 1:4). They were to return from the Mount of Olives to Jerusalem to wait. In the upper room the eleven disciples continued in prayer. With them were the mother of Jesus, the women, and his brethren (Acts 1:13, 14). Evidently others joined the worshiping group, for we are told that on the day of Pentecost there were about a hundred and twenty gathered (Acts 1:15).

Pentecost was a Jewish festival. The name means *fifty.* The festival was observed fifty days after the Passover holidays. It was a harvest festival which also commemorated the giving of the law on Mount Sinai by Moses. It was on the day of Pentecost that the Holy Spirit came upon all those assembled; note, not merely upon the eleven apostles (Acts 2:1–4). Note also that though Peter served as the mouthpiece, the other eleven disciples stood up with him (Acts 2:14). The revival that followed resulted in the forming of the first Christian church. Three thousand souls were the first fruits of this revival, and this number was rapidly increasing day by day by "those that were saved" (Acts 2:41, 47).

3. *The Jerusalem church.* These Pentecost converts were Jews. They read the Hebrew Sacred Scriptures (Acts 7:42, 43), they observed the daily periods of temple prayers (Acts 3:1), they kept the Jewish Sabbath, they observed the Jewish rules of diet (Acts 10:14). In addition they met on the first day of the week to commemorate the resurrection of Christ. Each week they shared in a fellowship meal followed by the sacrament of the Lord's Supper.

4. *The church at Antioch.* The Jerusalem congregation was the mother church. As time went on other congregations outside of Jerusalem were organized. The first daughter church of which we have a record was the one at Antioch. The persecution of the Jewish Christians by the antagonistic Jewish leaders caused the Christian converts to seek safety outside of Jerusalem. These religious exiles continued the ministry of the newly formed Jerusalem Church, preaching to Jewish people wherever they found them. At Antioch there were converts also among the Grecian Jews (proselytes). When the leaders of the mother church learned about the Antioch ministry, they sent a representative, Barnabas, to investigate. He was impressed by the gospel ministry in Antioch and remembering the Christian convert, Saul of Tarsus, who had not been well received in Jerusalem, Barnabas went to Tarsus, found the rejected and no doubt dejected Saul and brought him to Antioch. For a whole year Barnabas and Saul worked together at Antioch. It was here that the term "Christian" originated (Acts 11:26). The daughter church, Antioch, sent famine relief to the Christians in Judea, thus to the mother church. The once rejected Saul together with Barnabas brought this relief to Jerusalem (Acts 11:29, 30). It was from Antioch that the first missionaries were sent forth.

III. *The Growth of the Church.*

1. *Numerically.* The three thousand that were converted at Pentecost were but the beginning of the revival that swept Jerusalem. This included women as well as men (Acts 5:14). Even some of the priests were converted (Acts 6:7). Thus the membership of the Jerusalem Church grew. If numerical growth is a sign of success, the Jerusalem Church was a success. But increase in membership also increases problems which we will discuss later.

2. *Geographically.* The persecution of the Jewish converts by the Jewish religious leaders proved to be a blessing in disguise. The persecuted converts scattered through Judea and Samaria even as far as Phoenicia, Cyprus, and Antioch. They brought the gospel of Christ wherever they went. From Antioch, Barnabas and Saul

were sent by the church to bring the gospel to Jews living in other lands. Eventually the influence of the new movement reached through the outskirts of the Roman empire to the city of Rome, the very heart of the empire. Thus in less than half a century the Christian church had expanded from Jerusalem to Rome.

3. *Racially.* The members of the Jerusalem Church were Jews with a plus. That plus was the acceptance of Jesus of Nazareth as Messiah and Lord. Among these early Jewish Christians were Grecian Jews, Greeks who had become proselytes to Judaism, adopting its ceremonial rites and rituals. Although of another race, they had adopted the Jewish religion.

The first gentile convert to Christianity was an Italian military officer, Cornelius, stationed at Joppa (Acts 10:1). The Apostle Peter administered Christian baptism to the converted Cornelius and his household. Philip, the evangelist, likewise instructed the Ethiopian in the Christian faith and baptized him. It is possible that he already was a proselyte to Judaism, since he was reading the Hebrew Scriptures (Acts 8:32, 33). The real problem of prerequisites for becoming a Christian arose when Paul began to minister to gentiles as well as to Jews. The matter was settled once for all at the Jerusalem Council. A gentile need not become a proselyte to Judaism in order to become a Christian (Acts 15:28, 29).

4. *Organizational growth.* The Jerusalem Christians at first lived like a large happy family, a sort of communal life. Personal property and lands were sold, and the money was pooled in a common treasury (Acts 2:4, 5; 4:32–35). The first division of labor seems to have come as the result of a complaint. The Grecian-Jew-Christians murmured because their widows seemed to be neglected in the daily distribution of supplies. The apostles called a meeting to consider the complaint; the result was that it was decided that seven men should be carefully selected and ordained to the function of supervising the daily distribution from the common store. The apostles were to devote themselves to the gospel ministry. We have come to call these seven *deacons;* their function was, however, more like that of our present church trustees, men concerned with the material possessions of the local church.

As new needs arose more specialized workers were recruited. In his epistles Paul refers to bishops, deacons, and elders, as well as apostles, prophets, teachers, and so forth (I Cor. 12). By the end of the first century, the church had developed quite an extensive organization based upon the growing needs of an expanding church.

IV. *The Divided Church.*

Wherever a group of human beings live together and share

experiences, there will be differences of opinion and there will be tensions, whether it be in a family, a congregation, or a state. The first Christian church was not a perfect organization; there were tensions and animated debates. Even while Jesus was with his disciples, there was dissension within their group. There was the discussion of who were the greatest, who deserved special places of honor; even at the last Passover meal we find rivalry and contention. The church at Corinth was not only split, it was quartered (I Cor. 1:10–17).

1. *Gentile problem.* As the church reached out into the gentile world there was for a time a sharp cleavage among the Christians themselves as to policy. Should these Gentiles also become Jewish proselytes? So taught the Judaizing teachers. This view seems to have been favored by Peter, but strongly opposed by Paul. At the Jerusalem Council where James, the brother of Jesus, presided as moderator, the matter was finally settled in favor of Paul's point of view (Acts 15:1–35).

2. *The Protestant Reformation.* There were a number of theological controversies, too many to discuss in a survey of this type. The church became divided into an eastern and a western church, the Greek Orthodox and the Roman Catholic.[4] A deep and definite cleavage within the Roman Catholic Church was brought about through the Protestant Reformation. From its very origin the Protestant Church lacked unity. Luther, Melanchthon, and Calvin were strong personalities with deep convictions. They did not see eye to eye. Like bees, the Protestants have swarmed time and again; as a result we now have more than two hundred and fifty Protestant denominations and sects.

V. *Causes for These Divisions.*

A number of factors have contributed to these divisions within Protestantism. In many instances it has been the dynamic personality of individual leaders who have attracted a large following. After the death of the leaders, the groups have chosen other leaders and have carried on. In other instances there have been doctrinal differences based upon the interpretation of Scripture passages. In still others it has been the forms of worship and patterns of church organization and administration. The origin of some denominations has been in terms of race or nationality. There are African Methodist Episcopal Churches as well as Colored Methodist Epis-

---

[4] In 1054 A.D. the church was divided into an Eastern and a Western Church (Greek Orthodox and Roman Catholic).

copal Churches, also a Colored Primitive Baptist group, just to name a few.

Some denominations came into being to minister to immigrants such as German, Dutch, Swedish, Norwegian, Danish, and Finnish. At first all of the services in these immigrant churches were conducted in the language of the land from which the immigrants had come. Gradually as the immigrants' children became identified with the church, the worship became bilingual. With the passing of the immigrant generation, the language of the worship became English. Several of these denominations changed their corporate name so as to drop the suggestion of a foreign affiliation. The Swedish Lutheran Church became Augustana Evangelical Lutheran. The Norwegian Lutherans became Evangelical Lutherans. The Swedish Baptists became the Baptist General Conference. A few groups have retained their European heritage, thus Finnish Evangelical Lutheran (Suomi Synod), the Finnish Apostolic Lutheran, Slovak Evangelical Lutheran. The Danish Evangelical Lutherans have recently voted to omit the word Danish from the name of their synod. When the Norwegian Free Church and the Swedish Free Church merged in 1950 they omitted any reference to foreign affiliation and became the Evangelical Free Church.

In the United States of America we have denominations that still preserve the scars of the Civil War, although it is nearly a century since the close of that bitter struggle. Politically the states are united into one nation, but the church continues to be divided into a *North* and a *South*. The Baptists and Presbyterians are still separated by the old Civil War traditions. The Methodists have succeeded in bridging the gap and have effected a union between the south and the north.

As Christians we direct our theological thinking and our daily conduct from a common Bible, we pray to the same God, we claim the same Christ as our Savior, and we hope for a common heaven. Yet our church is not merely divided; it is splintered.

Denominations have their place in the organizational pattern of the Christian church. We need them. A certain amount of wholesome competition between denominations is stimulating, but when it deteriorates into rivalry and conflict, the denominations may become a detriment to the progress of the church. Yes, we need denominations, but do we need two hundred and fifty such separate denominations or sects? Could we not get along nicely with less?

VI. *The Mission of the Church.*

Following our superficial survey of the history of the Christian church we face the problem of orientation. After nineteen centuries of growth, development, and change, is the twentieth-century church doing what it should be doing? The student who has dedicated his life to the service of Christ and the church is concerned, not to say confused. There are so many patterns, so many deviations.

The church of today differs in many respects from the apostolic church. Is this as it should be, or has the church gone off on detours? The return to the pattern of worship of the early church would not be desirable, nor even possible. Even within the framework of time represented by the New Testament we find that changes took place. When a new need arose, a new agency was set up to care for that need. The calling of seven men to serve as deacons in the Jerusalem church was a response to a need (Acts 6:1–6).

Every living organism must conform to change if it is to survive. The church is a living organism. It too must adjust itself to the needs and conditions of each generation. But all change is not good; there are some changes that are detrimental to health and progress. How shall we evaluate the changes that have taken place?

The New Testament does not present a model constitution to govern the Christian church, but it does contain guiding principles. If we accept the Apostle Paul's definition, or analogy, that the church is the body of Christ and Christ is its head, we conclude that the mission of the church is to continue the ministry Christ was engaged in during his incarnation. For the objectives, the mission of the church, we turn therefore, not to modern philosophy, psychology, and sociology, but to New Testament theology. Our method of work, however, will be modified by our understanding of human nature, thus philosophy, psychology, and sociology become assistants rather than masters. We consult them, but they do not dictate to us what we shall do.

Charles M. Sheldon's book *In His Steps* was an attempt, and quite a successful one, at bringing the spirit and teachings of Christ into modern situations. *What Would Jesus Do?* was a subtitle given to that book. What would Jesus do if He were living here on earth in human form in the midst of our twentieth-century confusing world? A part of the answer will be found when we examine the gospel records of what Jesus said and did as He lived in a first-century world. Peter, one of the intimate disciples, describes his Master's ministry in simple terms: "He went about doing good, and healing all that were oppressed of the devil" (Acts 10:38). But "doing good" is perhaps too general a term to help us in delineating the functions of the church of today. Of what did this "doing good" consist?

The most commonly used classification of Jesus' ministry is three-fold: preaching, teaching, and healing. It is difficult to make any clear-cut distinction between preaching and teaching, nor is it necessary to do so, since both are concerned with proclaiming the gospel. In the introduction to the Sermon on the Mount, we are told that He "sat down" and "taught them" (Matt. 5:1, 2), while in the previous chapter it is recorded that Jesus began to "preach" (Matt. 4:17). Mark relates that Jesus suggested that they go to the "next towns" that He might "preach" there also (Mark 1:38). Jesus is more often referred to as a teacher (rabbi) than as a preacher. In fact, the term "Teacher" as applied to Jesus occurs forty-five times in the gospels.

As a teacher Jesus presented old truth in new form. He had not come to destroy the law, but to fulfill it (Matt. 5:17). His disciples were familiar with the Hebrew sacred Scriptures. Like Timothy they had from their early infancy known the sacred writings (II Tim. 3:15). But Jesus gave to these old truths new interpretations and pertinent applications. To his disciples He gave the command to "go and teach all nations" (Matt. 28:19, 20).

Jesus devoted much of his time to what we would call a "social" ministry. He healed the sick, drove out demons, fed the hungry, and raised the dead. He knew that the souls He wanted to save dwelt in mortal bodies subject to disease, that they possessed human minds, tormented by fears and frustrations. He knew that these individuals lived in social situations that were far from ideal. He knew that if the individual was to survive spiritually, the environment needed to be changed. The twentieth century church that would carry on an effective ministry must concern itself with preaching, teaching, and a social ministry.

But the three mentioned areas are not mutually exclusive; they are not fenced fields. There is and should be not only relating but integrating. The pastor who on Sunday morning from the pulpit expounds the Scriptures is not only preaching, he is teaching. When the Sunday-school teacher calls on an absentee pupil who lives in the slums, she is engaged in a social ministry as well as carrying out a phase of her teaching responsibility. Recognizing the importance of the sermonic utterances from the pulpit as well as the social workers' ringing of doorbells and calling at hospitals and sanitariums, we must in our survey limit ourselves to that function of the church which we commonly call Christian education, fully aware that it includes much more than recruiting and enrolling pupils in the church schools and preparing lessons and conducting class sessions. In the final analysis, Christian education embraces the entire work of the church.

REVIEW QUESTIONS

1. In what four ways is the term church used?
2. What is the origin of the church?
3. How did the Antioch church differ from the one at Jerusalem?
4. In what four ways did the church grow?
5. What problem was discussed at the Jerusalem Council?
6. Who were the speakers?
7. Who served as moderator?
8. How was the matter settled?
9. Who was the leader in the Protestant Reformation?
10. What were the results of this Reformation?
11. What were some of the causes of the rise of denominations?
12. Give examples of nationality differences.
13. How did the Civil War effect denominations?
14. How may the modern church know what it is to do?
15. What is the threefold mission of the church?
16. Was Jesus best known as a *preacher* or as a *teacher?*
17. What does the word *Rabbi* mean?
18. Were the disciples commanded to preach or to teach?
19. What is meant by a social ministry?
20. Give instances of a social ministry in the life of Jesus.

QUESTIONS FOR DISCUSSION

1. Evaluate the statement, "We must return to the pattern of the Jerusalem church."
2. What do you understand by a *homogeneous* congregation?
3. In what respects is the work of the church more effective when it ministers to a homogeneous group?
4. What are the advantages of having a variety of nationalities in one church?
5. What was the contribution of the foreign-language immigrant churches?
6. What is the objection to continuing them as foreign-language churches?
7. What is the difference between the *social ministry* of the church and the *social gospel?*
8. Why do so many Christians object to the term *social gospel?*

9. How would you characterize the ministry of such organizations as the Salvation Army?
10. What is your denomination and your local church doing by way of a social ministry?

3

Philosophies of Christian Education

STUDY OUTLINE

I. *Definition.*

Many devout Christians consider philosophy as dangerous to spiritual life. This fear is based on Paul's warning to the Colossians: "Take heed lest there shall be any one that maketh spoil of you through his philosophy" (Col. 2:8). They have failed to read the entire sentence, which concludes with the phrase "and not after Christ." Philosophy is not a hindrance but a help in organizing our Christian thinking.

Philosophy is an attempt to think consistently about life as a whole. The term *philosophy* means *a lover of wisdom*. We read that: "The fear of the Lord is the beginning of wisdom" (Ps. 111:10). Philosophy is to the structure of human thought what mortar is in the erection of a building — it holds things together. A pile of bricks is not a building, nor is an array of facts knowledge. The bricks need mortar, and the facts need a philosophy.

Philosophy is not limited to the disciplined thinking of a college classroom. The average man we meet on the street has a philosophy of life, whether he dignifies it by that name or not. Even the "tramp" has a philosophy. The guiding principles of our life constitute our philosophy. Science is concerned with the *what* and *how,* philosophy with the *why.* It was Francis Bacon who remarked: "A little philosophy inclineth man's mind to atheism, but depth in philosophy bringeth men's minds about to religion." Jesus said: "Ye shall know the truth, and the truth shall make you free" (John 8:32). The poetical books of the Old Testament have much to say about wisdom (Eccles. 2:13, 14; Job 36:5; Prov. 3:13).

II. *Philosophies of General Education.*

In the early history of the traditional normal school, where public school teachers were trained, no serious attempt was made to expound a philosophy of education. The few experts who prepared the curriculum knew, or thought they knew, the *why* of the pedagogical practices that were prescribed for the candidates of the teaching profession. The future teachers were coached in *what* to do when they found themselves in a teaching situation in a classroom. The duty of the teaching cadets was to *do or die* without questioning the reason *why.* Their training has been described as a matter of being given a bag of pedagogical tricks and then being instructed in how to use them. Perhaps with the limited time devoted to teacher training in those days this coaching was the most effective method.

The modern Teachers' College presents the *why* as well as the *how* of teaching. Courses in the philosophy of education constitute a core part of the curriculum. Progressive education has made familiarity with its basic philosophy a necessity. What Comenius, Rousseau, Pestalozzi, Herbart, and Froebel contributed by way of educational philosophies in the earlier centuries, John Dewey, William Kilpatrick, and Harold Rugg contributed to the educational philosophies of the first half of the twentieth century. These educational philosophies are never permanently fixed. They seem to be in a state of flux, changing with each generation. It should, therefore, not surprise us to discover that philosophies of Christian education are also subject to periodic changes. What is considered a good method in one generation may be outmoded, modified, or even discarded in the next generation. Wherever there is life there is change, whether it be in an organization or an organism. In secular education there is no one generally accepted philosophy but several, some of them differing from one another to an almost disturbing degree.

III. *Philosophies of Christian Education.*

Theology has been defined as the science of religion or science of God *(Theos)*. It is more properly a philosophy than a science. It is concerned not so much with the physical world as with metaphysics. The materials with which the theologian works cannot be measured by rulers, weighed on scales, or placed in test tubes.

The Christian church has been concerned with the formulation of philosophies of Christian education. Individual thinkers such as Walter Athearn, Norman Richardson, George Betts, William Bower, George Coe, and Herman Horne have, during the past half century, contributed books that have presented principles of guidance in the formation of philosophies of Christian education. Organizations such as the Religious Education Association, The International Council of Religious Education,[1] and the National Association of Evangelicals have appointed committees and commissions to study the entire field of religious education and to formulate governing philosophies. The Religious Education Association consisting of Protestants, Roman Catholics, and Jews found it necessary to generalize, in order to include all three faiths, to the extent that their findings have very little value in shaping a truly *Christian* philosophy.

A generation ago certain leaders in the field of liberal religious education advocated the divorcing of theology from the philosophy of religious education. Our educational vocabulary was to be purged from theological terms and in their place psychological and sociological nomenclature was to be substituted. Such words as sin, salvation, Satan, and Savior were to be deleted, for they were survivals from a prescientific age. Religious education was to become a substitute for evangelism. Religious thought was to be checked and modified by the latest discoveries in the field of science. The scientist and not the theologian was to be the judge of religious truth. Religious education was in danger of becoming humanism dressed in academic robes. The education proposed for the church differed very little from the character education offered in the public schools. The biblical content of the curriculum was

---

[1] Now: *The Division of Christian Education of the National Council of the Churches of Christ in the U.S.A.*

reduced to a minimum. The goal both in church and public school was to develop *good* girls and boys.

The dawn of the twentieth century seemed to promise a favorable day for social progress and economic achievements. Materialism and hedonism dominated secular living in church circles. Postmillennial theology was gaining ground. Moral conditions were improving to the extent that it seemed that the earth would soon be a fit place for the return of the King of kings. The first World War came as a surprise, but we survived. We shared in waging and winning a war to end all wars, so we thought. Graduates from Christian colleges and theological seminaries were going out to create a new world, a Christian utopia. Thus America lived in a fool's paradise until it was abruptly awakened from its beautiful dreams. First came the financial crash of 1929 which reduced millionaires to paupers almost overnight. There were those who had warned that financially fair weather would not last throughout the postwar day, but all such prophets of doom were discounted as pessimists. Then came the Second World War. We watched the war clouds gather in Europe, little dreaming that America would be drawn into the storm center. Then came that December Sunday in 1941 when the news of the attack on Pearl Harbor was broadcast throughout our land.

The humanistic liberal theology had neither anchor nor harbor to offer. Clergymen and seminary professors began to take an inventory of their religious stock-in-trade. A new orthodoxy came into being. A keen interest was aroused in the writings of Barth, Brunner, E. Stanley Jones, Niebuhr, and other Christian leaders. The Bible began to appear again in the curriculum of even liberal churches. Theological vocabulary was brought down from the attic of former discard, brushed up and put back into current use. This Neo-Orthodox movement made a great impact upon the general field of Christian education.

Religious education had become more concerned with methods of teaching than with the content. This gave rise to the Evangelical Teacher Training Association. It was founded by Clarence Benson of the Moody Bible Institute (1935). The movement, being non denominational, had a rapid growth. A publishing house, *Scripture Press,* was organized, and materials for Christian education were prepared, printed, and distributed. A number of other evangelical publishing houses came into being. This protest movement on the part of the evangelical churches caused the more liberal church-groups to reassess their teaching materials. The result has been that they too are returning to a biblical content in their curricula.

It was Immanuel Kant who said: "form without content is empty; content without form is blind." Theology is giving form to Christian thought. A curriculum of Christian education without theological content cannot be truly Christian.

But theologians differ in their views. In their thinking about religious matters they do not follow the same patterns. Even within the same denominational schools there are differences of theological interpretation. The Protestant policy of an individual interpretation of the Scriptures opens the doors to a variety of interpretations. Christians and Jews have much in common as to theology; so do also Protestants and Roman Catholics; yet there are material differences on vital issues. Within the Protestant church we have the two major currents of theology—Calvinists and Arminians. Calvinism is a system of theology and church organization that developed from the teachings of John Calvin (1509–1564). It stresses the sovereignty of God and advances the idea of divine foreordination and the individual's election to salvation. Arminianism arose in the Reformed Church of Holland as a protest against extreme Calvinism. It claims the free will of man. The name is derived from the leader of the movement, James (Jacobus) Arminius (1560–1609).

During the first half of the twentieth century, a movement arose in America which temporarily divided Protestantism into three groups—Modernists, Fundamentalists, and those affiliated with neither. It was not a controversy waged between denominations, but within them. It was a theological civil war. There were schisms within denominations, especially within the Baptist and Presbyterian denominations. Local churches were torn asunder and faculties of theological seminaries fought within their own ranks. Local churches, pastors, and faculty members were labeled as dangerous Modernists or as safe Fundamentalists. Theological books were weighed in the scales of orthodoxy. It was an open season for heresy hunting.

The majority of local churches tried to remain neutral. This third group watched the ecclesiastical drama, sometimes sympathizing with the one battling group, sometimes with the other, often with neither, and occasionally with both. The unchurched public watched this family fight within the church much confused as to the issues involved, and sometimes amused at the strategies employed.

Because of the influence of this theological controversy upon the philosophy of Christian education, it may be well for us briefly to review the origin and development of the movement. Since the liberal seminaries and church-affiliated colleges had courses in religious education and even departments of religious education, the very term *religious education* became anathema to the Fundamentalists. A radical change has taken place; in Bible colleges and Bible Institutes a great emphasis is now given to *Christian* education, its techniques, organizations, and underlying philosophy.

IV. *Modernism and Fundamentalism.*

Although the term Modernism has been widely used in Protestant circles, it originated in the Roman Catholic Church. Alfred Loisy (1857–1940), a Roman Catholic priest and teacher, published a book in 1902 entitled *The Gospel and the Church.* Loisy approached the problem from a modern scientific point of view rather than from that of the traditional theology sanctioned by the Vatican. He was first warned, and then excommunicated by the church. He taught for many years after that at *College de France.* In 1924 he wrote his autobiography, which was published under the title, *My Duel with the Vatican; the Autobiography of a Catholic Modernist.* Pope Pius X declared in a papal decree the teachings of Loisy to be heresy. On September 1, 1910, the Pope ordered every priest in the world to take the *Oath against Modernists.* Since 1931 it has been required that this oath be taken not only by the teachers at Catholic universities, but by all candidates for academic degrees. Thus the Roman Catholic Church built a retaining wall around its theology.

The term Fundamentalism was derived from a series of twelve books entitled, *Fundamentals: A Testimony of Truth.* These were published in 1910–1912, and circulated widely through funds provided by two wealthy laymen. In these booklets the doctrines listed as fundamental to the Christian faith were: (1) the virgin birth of Christ; (2) the physical resurrection; (3) the inerrancy of the Scriptures in every detail; (4) the substitutionary theory of the atonement; and (5) the imminent, physical, second coming of Christ.

These books became the standards for testing Protestant teaching and preaching. Borrowing the term Modernist from the Roman Catholics and calling themselves Fundamentalists, there arose within Protestantism a protesting group. The theological war waxed warmest in the Baptist and Presbyterian churches, although other denominations also felt the reverberations. Among the Baptists the battle centers were the divinity school of the University of Chicago and the Northern Baptist Seminary. Shailer Matthews was one of the leaders for the Modernists[2] and W. B. Riley became spokesman for the Fundamentalists.[3] Both Matthews and Riley were Baptists. Several new Baptist Theological Seminaries came into being in defense of "the faith which was once for all delivered unto the saints" (Jude 3) and as a protest against what was considered liberalism in the older seminaries.

In the Presbyterian Church, Princeton Seminary became the storm center. Professor John Gresham Machen, an able Bible scholar, led the revolt, which resulted in the founding of a new Presbyterian seminary, *Westminster,* in Philadelphia. The "Fundamental" Presbyterian churches organized into a reform group which since 1935 has functioned as a separate denomination under the name *The Orthodox Presbyterian Church.*

National and world-wide organizations of Fundamentalists were formed. Within the group of Fundamentalists there were theological bickerings and tensions. New groups were organized, until there was the Babel of doctrinal confusion. The National Association of Evangelicals is an attempt to bring the evangelical groups together. The American Council of Christian Churches is another movement primarily concerned with uniting the Fundamentalists in militant opposition to Modernism.

In present usage the terms *conservative* and *liberal* have come to be more common than the terms *Fundamentalist* and *Modernist.* A conservative theology strives to retain the spiritual values of the past without becoming enslaved to the traditions of the past. A liberal theology has but little concern for the past but addresses itself to the present and the future. But a theology is not necessarily known as only the one or the other, since there may be a *liberal conservatism* as well as a *conservative liberalism.*

V. *Theories as to the Moral Nature of the Child.*

Our philosophy of Christian education will be largely governed by our theory of the moral nature of the child. This is a theological as well as a philosophical problem. Throughout the centuries various theories have evolved.

1. *Natural depravity.* This view holds that the human race was by God created sinless but capable of sinning. Adam and Eve disobeyed the divine command and thus became guilty of sin. This

---

[2] Shailer Matthews was dean of the divinity school at the University of Chicago. His book *The Faith of Modernism,* Macmillan, 1924, presents the generally held view by that group at that time.

[3] W. B. Riley conducted his own Bible school in Minneapolis, Minnesota (Northwestern Schools).

sin not only separated the sinners, Adam and Ave, from God, but it contaminated the human race at its source. As a consequence the child is born sinful, because he is a descendant of Adam. Augustine (A.D. 354–430) expressed his conviction in the following words: "The infant who is lost is punished because he belongs to the mass of perdition and as a child of Adam is justly condemned." John Calvin, who lived twelve centuries later, held the same view. Children are born with inherited sin. Cotton Mather (1663–1728) exhorted his five-year-old daughter to "flee from the wrath to come." There are a number of Bible passages that have been used as proof texts (Ps. 51:5; Rom. 3:23; Rom. 5:12). The child is a child of Satan unless he has undergone the new birth.

One problem presented in this view is the infant who dies before he has become old enough to become converted. Two solutions have been advanced. The one is baptismal regeneration. The infant is born again in baptism. The baptized child is thus made a Christian through the sacrament of baptism. This is the view held by Lutherans and others. The other solution is expressed in the words of Calvin: "I doubt not that the infants whom the Lord gathers together from this life are regenerated by a secret operation of the Holy Spirit."

2. *Natural goodness.* The other viewpoint is that the infant is by nature good. If it becomes bad it is because of an unfavorable environment. This was the basic argument of Clarence Darrow, the attorney, in pleading the case of the two college students, Loeb and Leopold, who were charged with the murder of young Frank. Darrow made no attempt to deny the fact that the two young men had taken the life of the boy, but he argued that they were not morally responsible. Society was to blame for the crime, and if anyone was to hang, it should be society; and society could not be executed, only blamed. The result was that Loeb and Leopold were given life sentences in place of a death penalty.

The natural goodness of the child was a theory advanced by Jean J. Rousseau (1712–1778), the French philosopher and author. *All is good as it comes from the Creator; all degenerates under the hands of men.* It is reflected in *Christian Nurture* by Horace Bushnell (1802–1876) and his opposition to the then current revivalism.

The modern dictum of progressive education, "don't inhibit," is based on this theory and is fortified by the teaching of John Dewey (1859–1952) and Sigmund Freud (1856–1939). All the child needs in order to remain good is to be given the proper environment in which to develop. The infant is born without sin and needs neither conversion nor a Savior. If permitted to develop in a Christian environment, the child will gradually grow into a mature Christian. This is the general philosophy upon which the modern liberal school of religious education rests. The emphasis is on *nurture* since there is no need for a change of *nature*.

3. *Neutral nature.* A third view is that at birth the child is neither saint nor sinner, but as it continues to live and develop through its own free will, the child becomes the one or the other. There are neutral infants but no neutral adults. The natural urges and drives are God given and are in themselves morally neither good nor bad but are neutral. The infant is not from birth harnessed with the guilt of Adam's original sin. Adam's sin was atoned for in the death of Christ on Calvary (Rom. 5:12–21). The individual is lost not because of Adam's *sin* but because of his own *sins*. The effect of Adam's sin is reflected in the child's proneness to do evil rather than good, but that does not mean that the child bears the *guilt* of Adam's sin.

The infant is baptized, not to make him a Christian (baptismal regeneration) but as an act of dedication, for he already belongs to God. If the infant dies without having been baptized, he is still a child of His. The infant is from birth, not from baptism, a child of God (Matt. 19:14; 18:10). In some churches the baptism of the infant is admittance into the *fellowship of the church* rather than an entrance into the *kingdom of God*. He becomes a child of the church; he is already a child of God.

But what about *conversion?* Does the child brought up in a Christian home, nurtured in the Word of God, need a conversion experience? This will be discussed more fully in the chapter on educational evangelism. For the present our answer will be brief. Such a child needs a personal commitment to Christ in order that he may continue as a child of God. He must choose for himself.

VI. *Building an Individual Philosophy.*

From our previous discussion it is evident that we may not look for a unified philosophy of Christian education. There are, however, certain basic principles that may be advanced.

1. That the pattern of organization shall conform to the general organizational pattern of the denomination or local church.

2. That the content of Christian education shall be consistent with the theology of the denomination or local church.

3. That it shall conform to the generally accepted views of child nature and development.

4. That it shall recognize individual differences in local churches, in teaching staff, and in the members being taught.

5. That though it shall borrow greatly from educational philoso-

phy, from child psychology, and educational psychology, Christian education shall develop patterns and purposes that are distinctly Christian.

It is evident that every teacher active in the teaching ministry of the Christian church will find it necessary to tailor his own philosophy of Christian education rather than adopting the ready made. Existing patterns will offer worth-while suggestions, but each teacher needs a philosophy he can truly call his own.[4]

REVIEW QUESTIONS

1. How have Paul's words regarding philosophy been misinterpreted?
2. What is philosophy?
3. What did Francis Bacon say about it?
4. How did the early normal schools differ from modern teachers' colleges?
5. Name five early educational philosophers.
6. Name three recent ones.
7. What is theology?
8. Why is it more properly classified as philosophy rather than as science?
9. Name five Christian-education philosophers of the past half century.
10. What was the general spirit in America at the turn of the century?
11. How was Christian education influenced by this spirit?
12. What caused America to become alerted to conditions?
13. Name four modern leaders in religious thought.
14. How do Calvinism and Arminianism differ?
15. Where did the term *Modernism* originate?
16. What is the origin of the term *Fundamentalism?*
17. Who were the leaders in the controversy within the Protestant church?
18. What two denominations became theological storm centers?

---

[4] The following books will be found helpful:
    a. Bower, William, *Christ and Christian Education.*
    b. Bushnell, Horace, *Christian Nurture.*
    c. Chave, Ernest, *A Functional Approach to Religious Education.*
    d. Harner, Nevin, *The Educational Work of the Church.*
    e. Horne, Herman Herrell, *The Philosophy of Christian Education.*
    f. Richardson, Norman, *The Christ of the Classroom.*
    g. Vieth, Paul, *The Church and Christian Education.*

19. What is meant by *baptismal regeneration?*
20. What are the three theories as to the child's moral nature?
21. How does theology influence the philosophy of Christian education?
22. What was Calvin's idea as to an infant who dies?
23. What is meant by *total depravity?*
24. State five basic principles of a philosophy of Christian education.
25. How may a Christian educator build his own philosophy?

QUESTIONS FOR DISCUSSION

1. Of what value is an introductory course in philosophy?
2. Should we attempt to teach theology in the Sunday school? If not, why not? If so, at what age?
3. What are the chief dangers of an era of national prosperity?
4. How does the Roman Catholic method of curbing Modernism affect freedom of thought?
5. Did the Modernist-Fundamentalist controversy help or hinder the work of the Christian church?
6. Indicate ways in which you feel both groups were in error.
7. Give arguments for and against your church affiliating with either group.
8. Which of the three theories as to the moral nature of the child would you accept? Why?
9. Formulate a possible fourth theory.
10. Outline your own philosophy of Christian education.

4

Educational Evangelism

STUDY OUTLINE

Christian education is not a substitute for evangelism, it *is* evangelism. In popular thinking there is confusion as to what constitutes evangelism. To some it is a process of recruiting members for the church, to others it is an emotionally-toned, overt response to an invitation, to still others it means something else.

I. *Definition.*

Evangelism is not a biblical term, though the word evangelist is found both in the book of Acts and in the epistles. Philip is referred to as an evangelist (Acts 21:8). In enumerating the workers within the Christian church Paul includes the evangelist (Eph. 4:11). In his epistle to the young and timid Timothy, Paul urges the young preacher to "do the work of an evangelist" (II Tim. 4:5). We may conclude that evangelism is the main mission of the evangelist. *Evangelist* is a word of Greek origin and is derived from two words, the one meaning *good,* the other meaning *messenger.* An evangelist is a messenger conveying good news. The good news is the evangel. The four gospel-writers are frequently referred to as evangelists.

Gospel is an Anglo-Saxon word meaning *good news. Evangel* and *gospel* are thus synonymous, the one of Greek origin, the other of Anglo-Saxon. This gospel came first to the Jews and then to the Greeks (non-Jews) (Rom. 1:16). To the Jews the good news was that their long-awaited Messiah had arrived in the person of Jesus of Nazareth (John 1:45). To the Greeks it was that Jesus was the Savior of the world (Acts 15:16–18). Salvation was through Christ and was available for the people of all nations and tribes.

Evangelism is the process of spreading the gospel of Jesus Christ. It is not a specific act but a process. It is like a chain, each link a unit in itself uniting with other links to form the chain. The message of evangelism has remained the same through the centuries, but the methods of conveying it to others have varied.

II. *Evangelism Is the Mission of the Church.*

The purpose of the Christian church is to evangelize, to mediate the gospel. Christ not only proclaimed the gospel, he *was* the gospel. It is as we present Christ that we evangelize. When he ascended to heaven, Christ gave to his disciples a commission. We might say that it was his last will and testament. They were to go out and make disciples (followers of Jesus) of all nations, baptizing them and teaching them (Matt. 28:19, 20). It was a world-wide program of evangelism. They were to witness in Jerusalem, Judea, Samaria, and "to the uttermost part of the earth" (Acts 1:8).

If the church is to survive, each generation must recruit new disciples through the process of evangelism. It is often stated that the church is never more than one generation away from extinction. Its very survival is dependent upon evangelism. The book of Acts gives us a graphic description of the movement of evangelism in the church of the first century.

III. *The Specialist in Evangelism.*

Evangelism is usually considered the function of a gospel specialist, the evangelist. The evangelist, with perhaps a party of gospel workers, comes into a community or a local church. Like John the Baptist, the evangelist calls sinners to repentance (Matt. 3:1, 2). He gives altar calls and conducts "aftermeetings." During the campaigns the co-operating churches, or the local church, reduce all other church activities to a minimum, and everything becomes geared to evangelism.

Important as is the ministry of the evangelist, he would reap no harvest if it were not for those who have patiently and prayerfully prepared the soil and planted the seed. Christ reminded his disciples that they were sent out to reap where others had sown (John 4:37, 38). He suggested that the reaper and the sower should rejoice together (John 4:36). Parents, Sunday school teachers, and pastors have all had a share in preparing for the harvest, the hour of decision.

Walter Athearn, in discussing evangelism and religious education, pays a worthy tribute to those who share with the evangelists in the task of evangelism.

> When the lists of the names of the world's great evangelists are being prepared, I wish to ask a place on the roster for religious educators. I would begin the roster of great evangelists by recording first the names of all Christian parents whose godly lives and pious tuition had led their children to Christ; I would add next to these honored names the army of consecrated Sunday school teachers and officers who guided children and youth into a saving knowledge of God. Below these names I would add all others who had labored to bring men and women into the kingdom of God.[1]

In our age of specialization there is the tendency to depend upon the specialist. The church's program of evangelism becomes largely limited to these annual efforts. The local church has need of such special seasons. In the sense that they revive the spiritual lives of the Christians they are *revival* meetings. To the extent that they contribute to the extending of the gospel message to the unchurched they are *evangelistic* meetings. Whatever we call these special efforts, they meet a definite need in the local church.

Every sincere Christian regrets that professional evangelism has on occasion brought dishonor to the name of Christ, when the campaigns have become religious carnivals, when the gospel services have fallen into circus patterns, when psychological trickery has been resorted to in order to produce results. But we cannot afford to condemn the movement of evangelism just because it has been exploited by some for personal gain and glory.

No informed person would deny the impact made upon American life by such servants of God as D. L. Moody, "Billy" Sunday,

---

[1] *Character Building in a Democracy,* pp. 138, 139.

4 66 / 6

"Gypsy" Smith, William Biederwolf and others. Their evangelistic ministries are far enough removed from our mid-century era to make an objective evaluation possible. Nor would an informed person question that God is using such contemporary witnesses as "Billy" Graham. Mass evangelism is not, as some have contended, a relic of the past. The methods have been modernized, the patterns have been streamlined; but the gospel is the same, the objectives are the same, and the results are the same.

IV. *A Continuous Program of Evangelism.*

The local evangelical church must not limit its program of evangelism to such special campaigns and series of meetings, good as they may be. The church that would maintain its spiritual health must foster a continuous, conscious effort of evangelism. The gospel should be preached and taught with such clarity and conviction that any service may result in the conversion of sinners. The reason that we rarely have such experiences outside of revival meetings is that we do not expect such things to happen. In many of our evangelical Protestant churches both pastor and congregation would be very much surprised, not to say startled, if at the close of a Sunday-morning service someone would leave the pew and approach the pulpit with a request for prayer. If we preach and teach the gospel of Jesus Christ in the power of the Holy Spirit, such experiences should not be limited to revival meetings.

V. *Educational Evangelism.*

The primary purpose of Christian education is to make disciples (Matt. 28:19). The making of disciples is evangelism, thus Christian education is committed to the task of evangelizing. In Acts the followers of Christ are referred to as those who were "of the way" (Acts 9:2; 19:9, 23; 22:4; 24:14, 22). It is a significant expression. It denotes that they were moving forward, there was progress. A *way* is not a place where one stands still, but an area over which one travels towards a goal.

Evangelism and education fall into similar patterns, *knowledge, attitude,* and *action.* In evangelism there must first of all be information about Christ and the plan of salvation. Then there must be an awareness of one's sinfulness and the need of a Savior from sin. Finally there must be the response of the human will.

The prodigal son in the far-away land recalled the home he had thoughtlessly left. He had the *information* about it through past experience. He felt a desire to be at home again, even if it were only as one of the servants. He had a changed *attitude* towards his home. But nothing happened until he arose and went. Without *acting,* he could have starved to death in the strange land, even though he longed for the home about which he remembered so much. "He arose, and came to his father" (Luke 15:20). Father and son met, both had deep feeling which led both to action.

1. *Christian education is imparting information.* When the missionary faces pagan people on a foreign field, his first task is to learn the language of the people, so that he may teach them the fundamentals of the Christian faith. Before they can accept Christ as Savior, they must know who He is. Paul presents this problem in his epistle to the Romans: "How shall they believe in him whom they have not heard? and how shall they hear without a preacher?" (Rom. 10:14).

In the homeland we must likewise inform our children and youth about Christ and the gospel before we can invite them to commit their lives to Him. It is hazardous to put one's trust in a total stranger. Even the child born and reared in the pastor's family does not inherit religious information; he must acquire it firsthand. The mother and the Sunday school teacher who, in words the child can understand, relate the simple story of Jesus are contributing towards evangelism. The first step in educational evangelism, whether on the foreign field or in the homeland, is to convey information about Jesus Christ, and man's relationship to God.

2. *Christian education is developing attitudes.* Knowledge is necessary, but it is not enough. The Pharisees and scribes knew the content of the Law and the Prophets, yet they became the bitter enemies of Jesus. They plotted to take his life. They knew the letter of the law, but they refused to conform to its spirit. Paul contends that knowledge alone does not save: "The letter killeth, but the spirit giveth life" (II Cor. 3:6; Rom. 7:6). In writing to Timothy, Paul reminds his young friend that he had known the Scriptures since his early childhood, and that these Scriptures were *able* to make him wise unto salvation (II Tim. 3:15). The knowledge of the Scriptures was not equivalent to salvation. James, discussing faith versus works, declares that even the demons believe in the existence of God (James 2:19); they have knowledge about Him, but this does not transform them into saints; they still remain demons. Although knowledge is not salvation, evangelism must begin with information.

Emotions are the prime movers of life, according to psychologists. Only dead people have no emotions. God has created man an emotional being. Man loves, he hates, he is happy, he is sad, he hopes, he fears. True education does not curb emotions, it directs them. If conversion is to become more than a mere mechanical, muscular response to a stimulus, there must be an inner awareness of sinfulness and the feeling of the need of a Savior from sin. Only those who sense the guilt of sin are aware of any need of forgiveness. The intensity of the emotion is not what determines the reality of the experience; but true conversion must be more than the mere obedience to a command given by another, whether that be parent, teacher, pastor, or evangelist. There must be the inner response of the soul.

3. *Christian education is directed action.* Our emotions find expression in action. The frightened person runs away from that which frightens him; the angry person scolds or attacks that which annoys him. The happy person laughs, the sad person weeps. Our repeated actions develop into habits, and our habits control our lives. Attitudes are emotional habits. Reverence is a habit, so are also drinking, profanity, and gambling. There are good and there are bad habits. When an individual becomes converted, there is a new control, Christ control, which directs the emotions into constructive action. Man becomes a new creature, for he begins to live under a new management (II Cor. 5:17). Often we see gasoline stations, garages, and restaurants advertising *Under New Management.* The converted soul, whether young or old, operates under *New Management.* The self has sold out to Christ. This is the "new man" to whom Paul refers (Eph. 4:20–24).

Evangelism is therefore not alien to Christian education. It follows educational patterns; thus, they belong together. Evangelism is *a part of,* not *apart from* Christian education. The one is not a substitute for the other, nor are they in any sense antagonistic to one another. The question is not, does Christian education find room for evangelism, but rather, how may we in the best way promote evangelism within the framework of Christian education.

VI. *Educational Evangelism Must Be Graded.*

1. *The unity of the human race.* In the Declaration of Independence the founders of our nation recorded their belief in the unity of the human race in the words: "All men are created equal." The Bible supports this view. In Malachi we find the statement: "Have we not all one father? hath not one God created us?" (Mal. 2:10). Likewise Paul on Mars Hill declared: "And he made of one every nation of men to dwell on all the face of the earth" (Acts 17:26). Moffatt translates it: "All nations he has created from a common origin." Anthropologists agree that although human races differ in many respects, yet they belong to the same genus, Homo sapiens. All human beings seek happiness. The Declaration of Independ-

ence guarantees to all American citizens the right to the pursuit of happiness. It does not, however, insure the attainment of the pursuit. That which all men seek only a few find; but the urge to seek is universal.

All human beings have a capacity for religion. *Man is incurably religious,* in the sense that he finds no substitute that can satisfy the religious urge. Man reaches out for some being greater than self.

Man's sins as well as his virtues follow certain universal patterns. Primitive people are sin conscious; they torture their bodies in various ways in order to placate their gods. The conduct of the prophets of Baal at Mount Carmel reflects their fanatical earnestness in securing a rapport with their deity (I Kings 18:25-29). The forms of worship may differ widely, but the need is found in every human heart, whether it be a Hottentot or an American aristocrat.

2. *Individual differences in Christian education.* No two human beings are exactly alike. We sometimes say of twins that they are as alike as two peas in a pod. That may be true, for no two peas in a pod are altogether duplicates; there are some minor differences. When we observe human beings in general, these differences become quite evident.

a. *Differences in race.* Although they belong to the same genus, Homo sapiens, there is a striking difference between a black African and a blonde Scandinavian.

b. *Differences in temperament.* This is observed within the same family. Some members are always cool and composed while others are easily agitated.

c. *Differences in sex.* In early childhood there is but little differentiation of needs and interests based upon sex; boys and girls may be classified and grouped as children. With the dawn of puberty there develops a marked difference in interests and abilities.

d. *Difference in age.* Physical growth, mental maturation, social interests, and spiritual insights are a natural result of the experience we call living. The four-year-old, the fourteen-year-old and the forty-year-old may be members of the same family, eating at the same table, sleeping under the same roof, and worshiping in the same church; yet their interests, needs, and abilities differ greatly. It is the family that holds the group together.

e. *Differences in environment.* The radio, telephone, television, automobile, and rural free delivery have contributed much to bridge the gap between rural and urban environments, but there is still a striking difference between the congested metropolitan centers and the wide open spaces of rural communities.

Some children are nurtured in Christian homes, while others

grow up in the darkness of pagan American homes. The former
live in a Christian atmosphere seven days of the week, while the
latter have an hour's casual contact with religion once a week, and
some none at all.

f. *Differences in ability.* Some children are physically handicapped, while others have limited mental abilities. In our church-
school classes we will find some that belong to the near genius, if
not the genius bracket of mental ability, while others have below-
normal intelligence. The moron has an immortal soul the same
as the genius, and both need the same saving and keeping power
of the gospel.

The catalog of differences might be extended, but this should
suffice to impress upon us that our educational evangelism must
be graded. If we would be successful in our educational evangelism
we must recognize individual differences.

VII. *Children and Evangelism.*

Society is much concerned with child welfare. In order to care
for orphans and children from broken homes, orphanages and
children's homes are founded and supported. It has been said that
in America orphans are often better provided for than children
whose parents are alive. There is, however, one type of orphan
about which society in general gives no concern—spiritual orphans.
These children may live in beautiful homes surrounded not only by
the physical necessities of life but by luxury as well. Physically,
mentally, and socially they are well cared for, but spiritually they
are neglected and starved. With the psalmist they would have
reason to complain "No man careth for my soul" (Ps. 142:4).

This condition is not always due to carelessness or willful neglect.
It is sometimes a parental helplessness that comes from not knowing what to do. Even churches that regularly sponsor evangelistic
meetings seem uncertain as to the spiritual status of children. As
a consequence the program of evangelism becomes adult-centered.
Children conscious of being largely ignored in these evangelistic
efforts are inclined to think that Sunday school is for children, and
evangelism for adults, and that a child must have attained a certain
chronological age before he may become a Christian.

Chappell relates the incident of a little girl who at a revival
service was asked if she would not "come to Jesus." Naively she
replied, "I have never gone away from him yet."[2]

---

2 E. B. Chappell, *Evangelism in the Sunday School,* p. 90.

1. *Jesus' teaching regarding children.* Our final authority, as Christians, rests upon the teachings and example of Jesus. The gospels very clearly record his actions as well as his utterances regarding children.

   a. The small child is an example of what the adult disciple should be (Matt. 18:3).

   b. God is especially concerned about children (Matt. 18:10, 14).

   c. Children belong to the kingdom of God (Matt. 19:13–15).

   d. A blessing is promised for the one who "receives a little child" (Matt. 18:5).

   e. A curse is pronounced upon any person who causes a child to "stumble" ("who is a hindrance"—Moffatt) (Matt. 18:6).

2. *Christian "Nazarites" from birth.* Among the ancient Hebrews there were consecrated individuals called "Nazarites" or "Nazirites." The ceremony of consecration was inaugurated with a vow (Num. 6:1–8). For a certain period of time the devoted person was to observe certain rules of diet and of conduct. There were some who were born Nazarites; they were dedicated to God before birth: (a) Samson (Judg. 13:2–7), (b) Samuel (I Sam. 2:18, 19, 26), and (c) John the Baptist (Luke 1:66).

   There are Christians who in a like manner have been Nazarites (separated for God) from birth. Their mothers, like Hannah and Elizabeth, have dedicated their children to God even before they were born. Like Samuel, they have been brought to the house of God for instruction. H. Clay Trumbull, the founder of *The Sunday School Times,* in a book published in 1884, entitled *Teaching and Teachers,* wrote, "There are children of faith-filled parents who have been consecrated to Christ in faith-filled prayer from their birth, and who have been taught from their earliest knowledge to love and trust Jesus with all their hearts. They were never so actively in the service of Satan that they had any conscious struggle in leaving that service. Through the influencing power of the Holy Ghost they were brought into the hearty service for Christ before they had ever made a positive campaign against his cause. They cannot tell precisely when they were regenerated. They have no "experiences" of conversion to relate . . . But all this makes them no less truly Christian, no less regenerate children of God, than are their godly parents, or their devoted teachers, or their consecrated pastors."[3]

   That the children of conscientious Christian parents should, in

---

[3] pp. 346–347.

this way, be Christian Nazirites from birth seems to be the plan of God. What should be the normal, we have come to consider abnormal. It is contrary to the will of God that any of these little ones should have their souls soiled through willful living in sin (Matt. 18:14).

3. *Child evangelism.* *Child evangelism* has a worthy objective—that of winning children for Christ. Unfortunately, the movement has been blamed for the mistakes made by workers with a maximum of zeal and a minimum of knowledge and tact. Dealing with any soul is a delicate matter, and the soul of a child is especially sensitive. The desire to achieve *results* has often become more important than to evaluate what the lasting spiritual results have been. Children are easily influenced to act upon the leader's suggestion. Raising hands for prayer becomes a reaction of muscles rather than a response of the heart. To bring a group of children from non-Christian homes together and expect through object lessons and the memorization of a few Bible verses to bring them to a saving knowledge of Jesus Christ is neither biblical nor an evangelical procedure. The criticism of the Child Evangelism movement we offer is not directed against its motive, but rather against its methods.

Children's meetings may be very effective if they are sponsored by a church or a group of churches, and if the "evangelist" understands child psychology and is able to bring the gospel message to the children on the level of their understanding. When such meetings deteriorate into a circus conducted in the church, with stunts of different kinds to hold the attention of the children, we would question if much, if any, of spiritual significance results. The attempt to secure a response from children in an evangelistic campaign, when adults fail to respond to the invitation, is taking undue advantage of the children, who fail to understand what they are doing. There are a *few* child evangelists who seem to have a divine gift of dealing with children. The most effective person to guide the child to Christ is, after all, the Christian mother and the consecrated Sunday-school teacher.

VIII. *Youth and Evangelism.*

Since youth is a flexible term, we will, for the sake of concentration, consider the range of twelve through twenty-four years of age. In churches conducting confirmation classes there is an excellent opportunity for educational evangelism. The historical facts of the Bible, learned in the preceding years of Sunday-school training, are reviewed and integrated. The basic doctrines are studied through the catechism, and the meaning of what constitutes Christian living and the organization and function of the church are discussed. The pastor, in addition to teaching the class, conducts a personal interview with each pupil. Decisions for Christ are made, and these "converts" are invited into the fellowship of the church.

The Sunday-school classes keep the high school youth under the influence of Christian teaching. There are other youth organizations sponsored by the church. One of the most effective means of winning youth for Christ has of recent years been the Christian summer youth camps.

The problem of conserving the results of youth evangelism is as vital as the matter of recruiting and winning youth. The losses the local church has sustained in its teenage youth is most appalling. What good will there be from recruiting a large number of small children into our Sunday schools if we lose them in their teens?

IX. *Adults and Evangelism.*

The greatest number of souls are won for Christ during childhood and youth, but that does not mean that the season for evangelism closes with the entrance into adulthood.[4] True, it is more difficult to win the adult than the child. It is also true that when a child is won for Christ, there is a life as well as a soul that is won. In the mission halls of the city slums the work is almost exclusively with adults, derelicts of humanity, rescue work rather than educational evangelism. But there are large numbers of respectable adults whose souls need to be saved from sin.

The men's Bible class lends itself to educational evangelism. Men who would shy away from evangelistic meetings and who rarely attend a church service, unless it is a concert or a program, will Sunday after Sunday sit in an adult Bible class and thus be exposed to the gospel. More evangelism may be taking place in these adult classes than we realize. The major problem in educational evangelism on the adult level is to secure a teacher who has definite Christian convictions, without being a bigot, one who has tact and insight, one who is deeply spiritual without being sanctimonious. He must be able to lead a discussion without losing his poise or temper. Men's social organizations (Brotherhoods) may be very effective in an indirect approach to adult evangelism. Christian laymen wield a great influence over non-Christians even in a social way.

Women's classes likewise may become agencies in bringing non-

---

[4] According to statistics, only two per cent of converts are over the age of twenty-four.

Christian women into contact with the gospel. Taught by a spiritually mature person with a wholesome outlook on life, these classes may be very effective in spiritually influencing the lives of young adult women (25 to 35 years of age). In city churches where office workers and other professional women may be reached, such classes could contribute much to the church's program of educational evangelism.

X. *The Teaching Evangelist.*

Norman E. Richardson in his courses in Christian education made much use of the term *the teaching evangelist*.[5] It is a thought-provoking combination of two words. *Teaching* suggests the method, *evangelism* presents the goal. The teaching evangelist instructs with the objective of bringing the individual of his class to Christ. Like John the Baptist, he brings the class to Christ, "the Lamb of God, that taketh away the sin of the world," in order that they may become Christ's disciples (John 1:29). The teacher not only prepares the way for the evangelist, the teacher *is* an evangelist. The twentieth-century church needs a revival of educational evangelism.

REVIEW QUESTIONS

1. Is the term *evangelism* a biblical term?
2. Is the term *evangelist* a biblical term?
3. What is the meaning of *evangel*?
4. What is the meaning of *gospel*?
5. What is *evangelism*?
6. What was Athearn's attitude towards evangelists?
7. Name four evangelists of earlier days.
8. Name two present-day evangelists.
9. What is meant by educational evangelism?
10. What is *graded* evangelism?
11. What evidence do we have for the unity of the human race?
12. Give examples of individual differences within the human race.
13. What are Christian Nazirites?
14. What are some of the dangers of child evangelism?
15. What age span includes youth?
16. How may confirmation classes contribute to youth evangelism?
17. Name some other agencies ministering to youth.
18. What per cent of converts are over twenty-four years of age?
19. Who are the adults?

---

[5] Norman E. Richardson, *The Teaching Evangelist.*

20. How may the Men's Bible Class be effective in evangelism?
21. How would you characterize an ideal adult-class teacher?
22. What contribution can *Brotherhoods* make to evangelism?
23. For what class of women may the *Women's Bible Class* be especially effective in evangelism?
24. What is meant by a *Teaching Evangelist?*
25. Who made effective use of that term?

QUESTIONS FOR DISCUSSION

1. Why do some churches stress evangelism more than others?
2. When may evangelistic efforts become harmful?
3. What is your opinion of the expression, *Every pastor his own evangelist?*
4. Is it possible to be a true Christian without being able to cite a definite conversion experience? Explain.
5. Cite instances recorded in the New Testament that illustrate *varieties* of *conversion experience.*
6. Do children dedicated to God by Christian parents before birth, born and nurtured in Christian homes, need to be *converted?* Give reasons for your answer.
7. What are the chief criticisms against the traditional *Decision Days* in Sunday school?
8. Why do so many Sunday-school teachers fail to bring their pupils into a *Christ experience?*
9. How would you meet the criticism that *the Sunday-school lessons are not evangelistic?*
10. How would you plan a program of educational evangelism in your own church?

5

The Curriculum of Christian Education

STUDY OUTLINE

I. *Definition.*

The word "curriculum" comes from the Latin word *curro* which means "to run." The curriculum is thus a "race track." Educationally speaking, it is the ground we must cover in order to reach our goal. The word "curriculum" implies activity, but activity without a goal is merely riding on a merry-go-round; you get off at the same place you got on. There has been movement but no progress.

II. *Objectives.*

In order intelligently to discuss the curriculum we must establish goals. Many years ago an attempt was made to formulate aims in general education. Seven such aims generally known as the Cardinal Aims of Education were formulated:[1]

1. Health
2. Command of fundamentals
3. Citizenship
4. Worthy use of leisure
5. Vocations
6. Worthy home membership
7. Ethical character

Still another related set of goals has been expressed:

1. Physical efficiency
2. Vocational efficiency
3. Avocational efficiency
4. Civic efficiency
5. Domestic efficiency
6. Social efficiency
7. Moral efficiency
8. Religious efficiency

Although educators have used different words in stating the aims of general education, basically they have been the same. It is the good citizen that becomes the "nth" product. We grant that our modern educational system has failed to develop the ideal citizen, but that may be the fault of the methods employed rather than the goal desired.

Christian education must also have specific goals. Someone has said that one of our American weaknesses is that *we aim at nothing and hit it with accuracy.* We may not always achieve, but we should know what we are trying to do, where we plan to go. Several years ago Paul H. Vieth rendered a real service to religious education through his research on objectives. He concluded that there are seven cardinal objectives acceptable to religious educators in most denominations. He formulated them as follows:[2]

1. To foster in growing persons a consciousness of God as a reality in human experience, and a sense of personal relationship to him.
2. To lead growing persons into an understanding and an appreciation of the personality, life, and teachings of Jesus Christ.
3. To foster in growing persons a progressive and continuous development of Christlike character.

---

[1] F. G. Bonser, *The Elementary School Curriculum.*
[2] *Objectives in Religious Education,* pp. 80–88.

4. To develop in growing persons the ability and disposition to participate in and contribute constructively to the building of a social order embodying the ideals of the fatherhood of God and the brotherhood of man.
5. To lead growing persons to build a life philosophy on the basis of a Christian interpretation of life and the universe.
6. To develop in growing persons the ability and disposition to participate in the organized society of Christians — the church.
7. To effect in growing persons the assimilation of the best religious experience of the race as effective guidance to present experience.

These seven objectives may be abbreviated as follows:
1. God awareness
2. Christ awareness
3. Character growth
4. Christian society participation
5. Christian cosmogony
6. Christian church participation
7. Christian philosophy of life[3]

An eighth objective, participation in family life, has been added.

III. *Score Card for Evaluating Curriculum (C. C. Peters).*

The following criteria for evaluating the curriculum has been proposed by C. C. Peters:[3]

1. Fitness of materials to appeal strongly to pupils of the age for which the lesson is intended.
2. Fitness of the materials to meet the needs of the pupils as defined by child psychologists and sociologists (age levels considered).
3. Fitness to meet the specific objectives of the particular church (or other group) for which the materials have been prepared.

This three-item score card may not suffice for a critical evaluation, but it is helpful in making a general appraisal of the curriculum.

IV. *Denominational Objectives.*

Denominations have worked out their own objectives. In 1947 the Presbyterian Church U.S.A. adopted as the goals of Christian education the following:[4]

---

[3] *Indiana Survey of Religious Education*, Vol. 2, p. 114.
[4] *Christian Education in our Church*, p. 9.

1. To secure personal commitment to Jesus Christ as Savior and Lord:
    a. Through teaching little children the love, wisdom, and power of the heavenly Father, and their relation to Him, to his Son Jesus, and to his people.
    b. Through guiding youth and adults to accept Jesus Christ as their Savior and Lord.
2. To foster individual growth in Christian discipleship:
    a. Through worship — the development of private devotional living.
    b. Through study — an ever increasing knowledge of God and His will, through the study of the Scriptures and all known truth.
    c. Through recreation — relaxation, wholesome play, and appreciation and enjoyment of the good, the true, the beautiful.
    d. Through service — personal vocation; practice of stewardship and Christian citizenship.
    e. Through fellowship — Christian literature, family life.
3. To foster growth in the understanding and appreciation of, and full participation in, the beloved community — the Christian church and the Kingdom of God.
    a. Through group worship — prayer, hymns, sacraments, sermons.
    b. Through group discipline and study.
    c. Through fellowship with others of various Christian heritage, culture, and talents.
    d. Through co-operative action for achieving the spread and application of the gospel.
    e. Through active participation in developing Christian discipleship.

The objectives as articulated by Vieth have a strong social emphasis but are somewhat lacking in their gospel application. There is no reference to the Holy Spirit, though the other two persons of the Trinity are stressed. The Presbyterians, in their ultimate objectives referred to above, have stressed the personal commitment to Christ without neglecting the social aspects of the Christian life.

The Evangelical Covenant Church of America, which is a denomination conservative in theology and progressive in education, through its Board of Youth Work made a careful study of objectives as it was in the process of revising its curriculum of Christian education. A special Curriculum Committee was appointed. The objectives presented by Vieth were considered, and in conference with him the committee prepared a revised set of objectives suitable to the specific needs of its own denomination. These objectives were adopted by the Youth Board in 1950 and thus became the guiding principles for the future curriculum building.

OBJECTIVES IN CHRISTIAN EDUCATION

GOD
: 1) To develop in every child, youth, and adult, a consciousness of *God;* to develop an active faith in Him as a reality in human experience and to foster a sense of personal relationship to Him.

JESUS CHRIST
: 2) To develop in every person a growing faith in *Jesus Christ,* the Son of God, and to lead him to a personal acceptance of Christ as Savior and Lord.

HOLY SPIRIT
: 3) To develop in each person an awareness of the active presence of the *Holy Spirit,* the third person of the Trinity.

BIBLE
: 4) To develop in all persons a belief in the *Bible* as the inspired Word of God and as the perfect guide to Christian life and conduct.

CHRISTLIKE CHARACTER
: 5) To develop an increasing understanding of Christ's life and teachings which will result in continuous growth toward *Christlike character.*

CHRISTIAN HOME
: 6) To develop in all persons an understanding of the importance of establishing and maintaining a *Christian home,* and to live in the home according to the ideals and standards of Christ.

CHRISTIAN CHURCH
: 7) To guide individuals into an ever deepening communion with Christ and his followers through active participation in the *Christian church.*

Formerly the goal of education was thought of as filling the mind with facts. The good student was the one who could reproduce accurately the materials memorized. Before the printing press made the printing and distribution of books possible, this was an efficient

way of preserving, in retentive minds, the cumulative experiences
of the past. The printing of books now makes that method obso-
lete. Our modern view of education considers the curriculum not
as the goal, but as the means to an end. The curriculum is the
tool used to shape the individual personality and character. Tools
are necessary, but they are important only to the degree in which
they bring about the thing to be achieved. The best curriculum
will fail to achieve the educational goal sought if it is used by a
teacher who is unskilled or indifferent. Even a poor curriculum
may result in a gratifying product if taught by a good teacher. With
the warning that the curriculum is only an educational tool, we
will proceed to examine that tool.

V. *The Content.*

1. *Cumulative past experiences.* Life is too short even when it
includes the biblical three-score years and ten for an individual to
learn through firsthand experience the facts necessary for getting
the most out of life. The cumulative experiences of other generations are valuable in that they prevent us from repeating their mistakes. The achievements of the past will give us a sense of the direction in which we should move. Attempts in curriculum-building to ignore past experience and to focus only on current problems
have not been successful.

In Christian education there is a rich heritage from the past that
should be conserved and conveyed to the present generation. As
this heritage is transmitted through teaching there will be a screening process, since not all of the past learning is worthy of preservation. Then, too, there must be interpretations and applications in
order to make the past benefit the present and the future.

2. *The Bible.* History is a record of cumulative past experiences.
The historian collects data, selects that which in his opinion is
worthy of preservation, and then interprets these events and movements. Our Bible is sacred history. It consists of the record of God's
dealings with individuals and nations. The Bible begins with God
and creation. It continues with the story of man's creation, his
fall, and his redemption. This information is essential in a curriculum of Christian education. We do not limit the curricular content to the Bible, but the core of the curriculum should be the
Bible.

In curriculum-building the biblical materials are selected accord-
ing to the interests and needs of the learner. The language of our
English Bible is beyond the vocabulary of the small child, so the
Bible stories are paraphrased. There are in the book market a

large number of good Bible-story books for children. The use of colored illustrations adds much to the attractiveness of these books.

The writers of the Bible books did not have in mind a graded curriculum, nor a curriculum of any kind for that matter. They wrote these records for the benefit of other adults. The Bible is to be considered a *source* book rather than a textbook.

Unfortunately many of our modern youth have the idea that God was active through the Old Testament times and continued to be so in the New Testament times, but then retired. That is, they think that the sacred story concludes with the last chapter in the book of Revelation. To them there is no connecting chain of events between the end of the first century of the Christian era and the beginning of the twentieth century. The words of Jesus need to be stressed, "My Father worketh even until now, and I work" (John 5:17). There is need for a rapid and interesting survey of church history. In our present program of Christian education the fascinating records of church history are reserved for the curricula in our theological seminaries, but are not provided as curriculum material for the average Christian. Church history may be presented in a drab and boring fashion, but it may also become animated as one discovers the hand of God guiding individuals and nations through the centuries from Bible times to our own day. There is need for a popular course in church history that could be used effectively in Sunday-school curricula.

3. *Worship.* Worship is an awareness of the presence of God and a bringing of adoration to Him. Unfortunately, worship has sometimes become mechanized until it is little more than a parrot-like reading of responses. Litanies and responses may prove a help, but they may also become a hindrance. There are aids to worship, such as worship centers. The Roman Catholic Church has developed such visible aids to worship to the extent that they have actually dominated the worship.

Other aids to worship include silence and meditation, used so effectively by Quakers. But these are by no means a mode of worship to be used exclusively by them. Silence and meditation may be used effectively in leading the worship of youth and even children. Among others much use is made of formal prayers, read from a prayer book or recited from memory. To some these may seem to be lacking in spontaneous spirit, yet in a formal service they may prove effective in creating and sustaining a spirit of worship. Our informal prayers, after all, do fall into a general pattern. If we had a tape recording of a score of spontaneous prayers offered in public over a year's time by the same person, we would be very much surprised, as we listened to them reproduced, to note the very definite pattern into which the prayer falls.

The great weakness in our Protestant evangelical churches is not in the preaching from the pulpit, but the inability of the man in the pew to worship. When we come to worship, the world is too much with us. We do not lack interest, we have interest in too many things. We lack the discipline of concentration, because we have never learned how to use it.

4. *Music.* Music has always played an important role in the life of man, whether it be in war or in worship. In the Jewish temple worship there was much attention paid to singing. Our book of psalms was the temple hymnal. In the temple of Solomon the sons of Asaph were set apart as the official temple singers and musicians (I Chron. 25:1–31). When the Jews returned from the Babylonian captivity, the singers are given special mention (Ezra 2:41). The early Christians sang. Paul not only admonished the Christians to sing (Eph. 5:19; Col. 3:16), but when he was in prison at Philippi, he and Silas sang until the gates of the prison opened (Acts 16:25). In Luke we find included in the prose narratives poetical excerpts which were no doubt a part of the early Christian form of worship (Luke 1:46–55; 68–79).

The present age of jazz music with its resultant jazz living is wielding its influence even on the worship of the church. The church choirs labor with anthems, the offertory is classical music, the hymns sung in the Sunday-morning service are the traditional conservative hymns. But in Sunday school the children are taught to sing catchy gospel jingles. At youth gatherings our young people sing with happy faces and with feet beating the rhythm of some of the latest jazz music, set to sentimental religious words. When youth leaders are asked *why,* they reply, "That's what young people of today like." The question may well be asked, Why do they like it? Is it that they dislike the good old hymns of the church, or is it that they have cultivated a taste for the inferior type? Why should we not cultivate a taste for the superior type of music?

Directors of church music are often responsible for the attitude of modern youth to the hymns of the church. With their cultivated taste for classical music and the great hymns of the church, these leaders often fail to recognize that children and young people are not intellectually and emotionally mature enough to appreciate and understand what these musical leaders have to offer. Between the heavy traditional music of the church and the modern religiously superficial jazz gospel jingles, there is a large field that needs careful cultivation. It is a tragedy when our adolescents in their high-school courses in music learn to appreciate the good and the beautiful, but when these same young people come to church they are exposed to youth programs with music patterned after the radio crooner and the public dance hall.

Martin Luther recognized the place of singing in religious worship. He wrote a number of hymns in German, the best known of which is "A Mighty Fortress Is Our God," which has become the marching song of Protestantism. He also wrote a Christmas song for children known as "Luther's Cradle Hymn" ("Away in a Manger").

Isaac Watts wrote a number of songs for children. The best known is his "Cradle Hymn":

> Hush, my dear, lie still and slumber,
> Holy angels guard thy bed,
> Heavenly blessings without number
> Gently falling on thy head.

When he wrote this song he was a middle-aged bachelor.

In 1763 Charles Wesley published his *Hymns for Children*, containing a hundred hymns. Though rather heavily loaded with theology, the songs became popular, probably because of the music rather than the words. The book went through several editions.

For evaluating gospel hymns to be used in Christian education the following criteria have been suggested:[5]

1. The hymn *tunes* should possess musical charm and beauty and should be suited to the developing vocal powers of the pupils.
2. The hymn *themes* should be suited in thought and meaning to the growing interests, needs, and capacities of the pupils.
3. Hymns must stimulate childhood and youth to their best living, to lofty ideals, to noble purposes, and to intelligent enlistment in the Christian enterprise.
4. Hymns must be suited in spirit, tone, and meaning to the occasion in which they are used.

Modern *singspirations* have become the object of both sharp criticism and generous commendation. They are usually held on Sunday evening, either in place of an evening service or after the regular service. It is a service of song. It is community singing, using gospel songs. Although planned primarily for youth, a few of the older people attend. Usually the youth of the different churches of the community meet together.

These singspirations may deteriorate into religious orgies, or they

---

[5] Betts and Hawthorne, *Methods in Teaching Religion*, pp. 454–457.

may become a spiritual force in the church. So much depends upon the leadership. Youth likes to get together; what better place could be found for youth to assemble than in the church? Youth likes to sing; why should they not sing hymns and gospel choruses? The songs should be carefully selected. To permit an audience of animated high-school students to sing whatever they choose may not be wise. Some songs have catchy tunes, but the words are overly sentimental, even sensuous.

A wholesale condemnation of gospel choruses is neither fair nor wise. Young people become rebellious when they feel that they are being thwarted. There are good choruses, the tunes are appealing, the words are definitely biblical. But there are others whose chief appeal is to the feet rather than to the head and heart. A singspiration is more of a religious pep-meeting than it is a worship service. The program of Christian education has need of both.

In our worship services we should strive to cultivate in our children and youth an appreciation of the great hymns of the church, hymns that will survive. Many of our modern gospel-songs are popular today, but will be almost forgotten tomorrow, for they lack survival value.

The use, in Sunday school and youth services, of a different hymnal from the regular hymnal of the church has some arguments in its favor. The regular hymn book of the church is bulky and difficult for children to handle. It contains so many hymns as to become confusing. A small hymnal is less expensive and easier to handle. It will contain some hymns not found in the church hymnal, suitable for children.

But there are objections. If youth sings its own songs from its own song book, will they not feel strange when they share in the regular church worship, singing strange songs from a strange book? The problem may be solved in part at least by publishing a hymnal for youth that contains a selection of hymns from the church hymnal.

5. *Art.*

Religious art is a graphic expression of religious ideas. The ancient Egyptians expressed their ideas of the character and activities of their gods in drawings of various kinds. The Greeks presented their deities in sculpture. The Jews were strictly forbidden by the Mosiac law to make any image of their god. Among the Romans (Italian) we find both sculpture and painting. The Roman Catholic Church has in its architecture and forms of worship made much use of art. The Puritans, reacting strongly to a cold formalism in worship, turned their backs upon any form of art and stressed simplicity. Their meeting houses were purposely bare and devoid of decorations of any sort.

The twentieth century has witnessed a return to the use of art in Christian education, even within evangelical Protestantism. Two brothers have contributed much towards stimulating and directing American Protestantism in introducing art into the curriculum of Christian education. One of these, Henry Turner Bailey, was until 1930 curator of the Cleveland Art Museum. His brother Albert was professor of religious art at Boston University. Two of his books are widely used, *Gospel in Art* and *Use of Art in Religious Education*. Recently two valuable books on Christian art have been published, *Christ and the Fine Arts* by Cynthia Maus, and *The World's Great Madonnas* by the same author.

The colored picture cards and large picture rolls used in connection with the International Uniform Sunday-School Lessons are familiar to teachers and pupils of a generation ago. The recent development of religious films, film strips, and slides has expanded the field of Christian art. The symbolism of the Christian church, as expressed in the art-glass windows and other appointments of the church, offer another field for the study of Christian art.

Prints of the masterpieces of art are available at practically all religious bookstores. A picture library may be built up with a minimum of expense. These pictures may be mounted, indexed, and filed in a cabinet to be used by teachers in different departments in the classes of vacation church schools and weekday church schools, besides in the Sunday school. Such artists as Copping, Da Vinci, Durer, Hoffmann, Hunt, Michelangelo, Millet, Plockhorst, Raphael, and Rubens could be represented in such a collection of pictures. There are contemporary artists like Warner Sallman known the world over for his "Head of Christ," Louis Jambor with his as yet not widely known "Jesus of Nazareth," and Signe Larson of Lindsborg, Kansas, who has given her interpretation of Jesus in a picture entitled "Thy Kingdom Come."

The Bible should be the core of the curriculum of Christian education, but there is available a wealth of resource materials to enrich the teaching ministry. In our enthusiasm for new and improved teaching techniques, we must not forget the importance of the content of the curriculum. In our use of extra-biblical materials we must strive to retain a truly Christian spirit. Education administered by and in a church may easily change in spirit so as to become a church-sponsored, glorified secular education. If it is to be Christian, it must be Christ-centered.

VI. *The Use and Abuse of the Curriculum.*

The curriculum is not an end in itself but a means to an end. It is an aid to learning. Some teachers want a curriculum that is planned in every detail. They like to conduct their classes along very definite lines, like a train running on the rails of the road bed. Others want flexibility in their teaching. They are conscious of a sense of direction, but they desire freedom in their teaching—just as in driving an automobile on a highway there are general limitations, but there is also room for a certain amount of freedom.

Some teachers become slaves to their curriculum. This is especially true in using "factory-made" curricula that provide questions and answers, illustrations, and so forth. In slavish use of such "factory-made" curricula, the teaching cannot help but become mechanical and uninteresting. The cry, "We want more lesson helps," reflects a lameness in the teaching profession; it is a demand for crutches. Lesson helps that give every detail of what the teacher is to do hinder the development of teaching proficiency. Some guidance is needed, but too much may prove educationally detrimental.

REVIEW QUESTIONS

1. What is the meaning of the word "curriculum"?
2. What were the seven Cardinal Aims of Education?
3. What is the value of aims in education?
4. Give Vieth's seven objectives in the abbreviated form.
5. What eighth objective has been added to the seven?
6. When did the Presbyterian Church U.S.A. formulate its objectives?
7. When did the Evangelical Covenant Church adopt its own objectives?
8. What were C. C. Peters' three criteria for evaluating the curriculum?
9. What is meant by cumulative past experience?
10. Why is the Bible a source book rather than a textbook?
11. What is worship?
12. What dominates Roman Catholic worship?
13. How does the Quaker worship differ from that of other Christians?
14. What is the difference between formal and informal worship?
15. In what way do informal services tend to become formal?
16. What use did the Hebrews make of music?
17. What use did the early Christians make of music?

18. What did the early Methodists contribute to music in Christian education?
19. What suggestions are made for evaluating gospel songs?
20. What is the purpose of a singspiration?
21. Who were the Bailey brothers?
22. Who compiled *Christ and the Fine Arts?*
23. Name some great religious artists of the past.
24. Name three contemporary religious artists.
25. How may a picture library be completed and used?

QUESTIONS FOR DISCUSSION

1. What do you consider the major weakness of Vieth's objectives?
2. Give your evaluation of the objectives formulated by the Presbyterian Church.
3. How do the Covenant Church objectives differ from the ones formulated by Vieth?
4. Would Peters' criteria apply to conservative as well as liberal curricula? Explain.
5. Prepare a worship program indicating the age group with which it is to be used.
6. Give a list of five gospel hymns you feel have survival value.
7. Name five popular gospel songs which you feel do not have survival value.
8. Name five good gospel choruses.
9. Name five that you feel are unworthy of a program of Christian education.
10. Name five examples of good religious art, giving the names of the artists and the titles of the pictures.

Methods in Christian Education

STUDY OUTLINE

I. *What Is Teaching?*

Education is sometimes referred to as a *science,* at other times as an *art.* It is both. Teaching and learning is governed by certain basic principles. These have by some educational psychologists been called laws, by others principles. These are provided by the Creator. Man does not make the laws of learning; he discovers and describes them. Newton did not create the law of gravity, he discovered it and formulated the terms which describe it. In this sense education is a science.

But education is more than a scientific research; it is creative, thus it is an art. The teaching process has sometimes been referred to as the work of an artist working with colors on the canvas of a child's mind. This is a poetic analogy, but it is not an accurate account of what happens. The canvas is passive and merely absorbs and displays the colors applied by the artist's brush. Learning, however, is not a passive but an active experience. Scientifically it would be more accurate, though less poetic, to use the analogy of a building project. The curriculum provides the materials and the tools, but the building is done by the learner himself under the guidance of the architect, the teacher.

True teaching is a matter of creating conditions that make it possible for another to learn. The frustrated pupil who remarked to his discouraged teacher: "You can't learn me nuthin'," spoke more truth than he realized. All the teacher can do is to provide materials and create an environment that is conducive to learning. The teacher learns as he teaches, but he learns only for himself. The pupil must do his own learning. In building a house it is not enough that good building materials are available, there is also a necessary technique, a workmanship. Likewise in education, the best of curricula may fail to produce the desired results if the methods of education are at fault. There is a right and a wrong method of teaching the Bible. Poor teaching methods and an undesirable educational environment may cause the pupils to develop a distaste for the Bible.

We have previously considered the curriculum and its objectives, the *What* of education. Now we come to the matter of methods, the *How* of education. The noblest of educational objectives will be useless, as far as achievement is concerned, unless we have an effective method of reaching our goals.

In his book *How to Teach Religion,* George H. Betts proposes four questions:[1]

1. What outcomes do I seek?
2. What material or subject matter will best accomplish this aim?
3. How can this material best be organized?
4. What shall be my plan or method of presentation?

He presents three outcomes or aims:[2]

1. Fruitful knowledge
2. Right attitudes
3. Skill in living

Bett's book, published more than thirty years ago, is somewhat lacking in modern educational terminology, but it deals with the basic facts of education as it applies to the teaching of religion.

---

[1] p. 42.
[2] *Ibid.,* p. 47.

The great advantage of the book for the average worker is that it is extremely practical rather than confusingly technical.

II. *The Teacher.*

Before we discuss methods, we need to devote our attention to the one who is to use the methods, the teacher. A good violinist can produce good music even when playing on an inexpensive instrument, but a poor fiddler produces poor music even if he plays on a Stradivarius. Curriculum and methods are both essential in Christian education, but when all is said and done, it is the teacher who is responsible for the success or failure of the teaching project.

Elmer H. Wilds, in discussing the world's great teachers, nominates three as, in his opinion, the world's greatest. They are Socrates, Guatama (Buddha), and Jesus.[3] He adds, "Jesus was undoubtedly the greatest of the three." In his further comments Wilds says, "In his personality, in his life, in his teachings, Jesus represented the ideal teacher."

But what about Jesus' methods? Did He make use of some secret technique unknown to Christian educators of today? A careful study of the four gospels indicates that the teaching methods Christ used were not different from those used by other teachers of his day. The parabolic method which He used so effectively was not a new method. The use of questions for ferreting out truth was employed by the great Greek teacher, Socrates, long before the time of Jesus. Any or all of the teaching techniques used by Jesus are available to the Christian teacher of today. It was the character and personality of Jesus that set Him apart as the ideal teacher. He not only taught truth; He was the truth (John 14:6).

Later in this course we shall consider the recruitment and training of Christian teachers. For the present we shall focus our attention on the methods of teaching. There is no one *ideal* method of teaching. There are a number of different methods. The choice of method will depend upon five factors:

1. The teacher's skill and interests
2. The curriculum used
3. The age of the pupils
4. The specific objective of the course
5. The environment and equipment

1. *The teacher's skill and interest.* There are some Sunday-school teachers who have had both technical training and experience in

---

[3] *The Foundations of Modern Education,* p. 146.

general education. For instance, a teacher who during the week teaches in the public school and on Sunday in the Sunday school would be interested in and be qualified to use methods that the average Sunday-school teacher should not even attempt.

2. *The curriculum used.* The curriculum will often decide the method to be used. There are courses prepared with class discussion in mind. Then, too, there are patterns of curricular organization, for instance the traditional *International Uniform Sunday-School Lessons* as compared with the new curriculum prepared by the *Presbyterian Church U.S.A.*

3. *The age of the pupils.* With small children the story method of instruction is used. In the adult class the lecture or the discussion method seems most effective. One would scarcely try the discussion method with a class of four-year-olds, nor the Bible story method with a group of forty-year-olds.

4. *The specific objective of the course.* It is not enough that we are conscious of general objectives in Christian education, nor that we have immediate goals for each lesson we teach; there should also be objectives for each course. What are we trying to achieve in these lessons? What changes do we hope will be brought about in our pupils?

5. *The environment and equipment.* If the teacher shares a large auditorium with half a dozen other classes, he cannot make use of audio-visual materials, such as a sound film, without interfering with the instruction in the other classes, nor can he use flannelgraphs without distracting pupils in neighboring classes.

III. *Motivation.*

The major problem in all education is motivation. It is evident that a person learns whether he is motivated or not, but he learns quicker and the results are more lasting when the learner is properly motivated. Take the case of a good Christian who works in a factory beside an ungodly person who swears. The Christian has no desire to learn these oaths, but he cannot help hearing them. He is exposed to these words day in and day out. He tries to push them out of his mind. After several years of thus being exposed to the fellow-worker's language, the Christian goes to the hospital for surgery. As he is emerging from the unconscious state caused by the anesthetic, he utters a whole volley of oaths. The assisting nurse, knowing that the patient is a professing Christian, wonders if he is a religious hypocrite. The psychological explanation is that the repetition of these oaths have been registered on his mind and pushed down into the unconscious mind. They are kept below the conscious level, but they are there. Under the influence of the anesthetic the controls have been temporarily removed, and the words that under normal conditions have been suppressed now find free expression. He had learned these words without wanting to do so.

Motivation is a matter of attitude, and attitude is feeling. The pupil who has had no interest in the study of the geography of the United States suddenly becomes interested when he learns that he is to accompany an uncle on an auto tour that will take him across the entire country. When pupils are motivated, learning is facilitated. Teachers, too, need to be motivated. The Sunday-school teacher who meets his class every Sunday merely because there was no one else to take the class is not motivated. On the other hand, the teacher who is vitally interested in the individual child, as well as children as a whole, is well motivated. Whatever method we use, both pupil and teacher motivation are essential.

IV. *Methods.*

1. *The story method.*

a. The *oral narrative* is perhaps the oldest method of instruction. Long before history was recorded in writing it was preserved in the form of the oral narrative handed down from generation to generation. The storyteller is an artist who sketches word pictures to be filled in by the imagination of the hearer.

With young children who have not as yet mastered reading, the oral narrative is especially effective. Much of the Bible can be taught in story form. Adults as well as children enjoy stories well told. The parables of Jesus were stories conveying spiritual truth.

The following suggestions may be helpful in effective storytelling:

1. The story should have action rather than description.
2. The events should be within the range of the hearer's experience.
3. The story may be simplified and modernized, but must not be distorted so as to change its original meaning.
4. Make use of direct discourse (Let the characters speak for themselves).
5. Work for a definite climax in the story.
6. After reaching the climax, stop.
7. The lesson, or moral, of the story should be so evident that the listener can make his own application.

b. *The acted narrative.* Primitive man makes much use of action in telling a story. The religious dance and the weird war dances of savages are stories acted out. Civilized man finds similar expression in the drama. Many religious educators advocate the use of the drama in teaching religion. Some of our Christian colleges have established departments where the techniques of the dramatic method are taught. Other Christian leaders are hesitant about approving the drama. They fear that it may foster a taste for the theatrical rather than the spiritual. They also warn that there is grave danger that reverence for the Bible is lost when biblical material is used in a play. An objective position to take would be to grant that the drama is *a* method in Christian education. It is one of the most difficult techniques to use effectively. In order to be truly educational, the story to be dramatized must be first of all carefully selected. Then its contents must be mastered to the extent that those who act out the drama feel the spirit of it. The rehearsals must be conducted in a reverent manner; Christianity is not a toy to entertain. Finally, the public presentation should be made in a spirit of worship. If after a dramatic performance the comments of the audience are limited to how sweet little Johnny looked, or how well Mary acted her part, it is a question whether or not the message of the drama reached the audience, or whether the message was not altogether eclipsed by the technique. In order to be effective, the preparation and presentation must be directed by a leader who not only knows the techniques of the drama, but who also has an appreciation of spiritual values.

A religious drama may be more effective than a preached sermon, but it may also be spiritually but a fiasco. Even those who object to the drama in Christian education do not object to dialogues representing biblical characters without costumes or stage settings. Small children are naturally dramatic as they represent birds, flowers, snowflakes, and so forth, in their action songs. The dramatic method in Christian education is not to be condemned, but to be used in a reverent manner to the glory of God by those who are trained and equipped.

c. *The written narrative.* Much of our Bible is in the form of history and the biographies of interesting characters. However, the Bible was not written for children but for adults. In order to convey these Bible stories to small children it is necessary to paraphrase them. Bible-story books with beautifully colored pictures are available at varying prices. They may be found even in the Five and Ten Cent Stores. Mary Alice Jones has written a number of fascinating storybooks for children; *Tell Me About God,* and *Tell Me About Jesus* are perhaps the best known. Of the books published earlier there are three that are quite well known: *Egermeier's*

Bible-Story Book by Elsie E. Egermeier, *Hurlbut's Story of the Bible* by Jesse Lyman Hurlbut, and *Child's Story Bible* by Catherine F. Vos. Long before they have learned to read, the children enjoy the pictures. They often retell the Bible stories they have heard read to them. They are usually not too accurate in the details and may transfer incidents from one story to another.

The Sunday-school materials for the nursery department are usually in the form of Bible and nature stories to be read to the nursery children by others. These pupils' books, besides having colored pictures, often have drawings for the children to color, usually with ordinary crayons. Sometimes this coloring is done in class, sometimes at home. The mother gets a refresher course in Bible as she reads these stories to her children.

2. *The lecture method.* The lecture resembles the oral narrative in that it is a one-way process, the teacher is active and the class passive. The teacher talks and the pupils listen. There is one major difference in that the narrative describes adventure, while the lecture may be an array of factual material. The teacher who merely rambles in his presentation is neither lecturing nor narrating.

For large adult classes the lecture may be the best method of instruction. A maximum of information may be presented in a minimum of time. It is used effectively in colleges and universities where students have been trained to the self-discipline of listening carefully and taking lecture notes.

The method does, however, have certain limitations. Altogether too often the teacher does both the talking and the thinking, while the pupils are physically present but mentally absent. The pupil who looks so very interested may be interested in something altogether foreign to the topic the lecturer is discussing. The teacher and the pupil are not on the same wave length. The pupils may be attentive and yet not understand the idea that the instructor is trying to convey.

3. *The recitation method.* The recitation has one advantage over the lecture. It is a two-way process, in which the teacher asks and the pupil answers. The answer was formulated by the author of the textbook; the pupil memorizes it and recites it as a response to the stimulus of the teacher's questions. The recitation has another advantage, and that is that the pupil must have prepared in order to be able to answer. Memorization is usually checked by means of recitation. The wise teacher using this method will ask the pupil to repeat the answer in his own words in order to insure

understanding, since the pupil may give the *right* answer, and yet not know the meaning of what he is saying.

4. *Socialized recitation.* This is a teaching technique in which the members of the class teach one another through the sharing of ideas and experiences. The teacher serves as a chairman to stimulate and direct the discussion. He may present problems for co-operative solution. For adolescent and adult classes this method of instruction may be very effective.

There are, however, certain inherent dangers in this method. A small, aggressive minority may monopolize the discussion. Individuals with theological axes to grind may take advantage of this freedom of speech. Then, too, the class period may deteriorate into a talkfest with the time largely wasted. The wise teacher will tactfully direct the discussion so that too much time will not be spent on trivial talk at the expense of a thoughtful discussion of vital issues.

In some classes a member is selected as a recording secretary to take notes on the discussion and at the close of the teaching period to present a summary. Where there is no such secretary the teacher should bring the discussion to a focus. If this is neglected, the effect of the discussion will be indefinite—a lot of talk, but no conclusions. At the beginning of each session it is well to spend a few minutes in a review of the previous Sunday's session. This helps to integrate the course.

5. *Problem projects.* We learn by listening, but we also learn by doing. It is often said that a lesson has not been fully learned before it has been put into action. In the problem-project method we not only think about what things might and should be done, but we *do* them. The thinking is done during the class session, while the project part, the doing, takes place outside of the class period. Social projects serve as expressional activities in courses that focus on Christian principles of living. The most common projects are perhaps the traditional Thanksgiving and Christmas baskets provided by some class, or other church group, and delivered to poor families. The opportunities for rendering Christian service in a social way by classes and church organizations are to be found in every church community.

6. *Manual-arts projects.* The term *manual arts* suggests that things are made with the hands. It is a creative art, a craft. The Sunday-school session is too brief to allow for the use of such arts, except with the smaller children who color pictures, and so forth. Then, too, these projects are usually of the type that would not be engaged in on Sunday. In the vacation church school, where the

time element is not a deterring factor, manual arts are very helpful in sustaining interest as well as in supplementing the eye-and ear-learning. Saturdays and after school time may also be utilized in these projects.

Without attempting to present a complete list of the types of manual arts, we will name three of the most common: (1) *Mapmaking.* This may be a group project where an entire class co-operates on one large map. It may be a map of Palestine, of the mission fields, or of the church community. These may be physical, political, or historical. The physical map would show mountains, rivers, and so forth. The political map would show neighboring territories, for example, Palestine and its neighbors. The historical map would show where historical events took place, for example, the missionary journeys of Paul, or Christ's public ministry. (2) *Modeling.* Sculpturing in soap or modeling with clay gives opportunity for creative art. Palestinian homes, shepherd's equipment, and sheep, are only suggestions of what may be done. (3) *Making and Lettering Scrolls.* This may be used as an incentive in memorizing Scripture passages. The pupil memorizes as he letters the scroll.

In Christian education we must maintain standards of perfection. To accept manual art work in the educational work of the church that would be rejected in secular education because of failure to measure up to standards of perfection is scarcely dignifying the educational work of the church. Then, too, there is the danger that the work becomes a teacher's rather than a pupil's project. The teacher should merely guide and evaluate. If the project is of such difficulty that the teacher must do a major part of the work, it has not been wisely chosen. There will be some pupils who will be more adept at hand work than others. Guard carefully lest the class project becomes the project of a small minority. Every pupil should make some worthy contribution towards the group project. The teacher will need tactfully to give the necessary guidance. Manual arts usually results in an untidy-looking room. The class should store the materials and tidy the room at the close of each workshop session. The teacher who herself does this chore for them is guilty of poor leadership.

V. *Audio-Visual Aids in Teaching.*

Although commonly referred to as teaching *aids,* audio-visual aids may properly be called *techniques* of teaching because of the combination of the word *audio* with the word *visual.* There are a number of such techniques or aids at the teacher's disposal.

1. *Nonprojected materials:*
   a. blackboards

    b. flannelgraphs[4]
    c. flat pictures
    d. maps and models
    e. worship centers

The above are visual materials. The teacher, through speaking, provides the interpretation and application of what the pupils see. The flannelgraph is a modern adaptation of the traditional blackboard. Instead of drawing characters with crayons on the blackboard, the teacher places already drawn, cutout pictures on the board, which is supported on an easel. The flannelgraph is an effective means of arresting the attention of children. In order to be of teaching value, the materials to be used need to be carefully selected to fit the age of the pupils. It is not advisable to use the flannelgraph at all class sessions, but an occasional use may prove helpful.

Worship centers contribute to focusing attention. A table with an open Bible, a cross, a pair of candles, or a picture of Christ can constitute a worship center. One or at most two objects should occupy the table. Using several objects at the same time tends to distract rather than to focus attention. With young children a picture of Christ placed on a table may serve as an effective worship center. In teaching or leading the worship, the teacher should carefully avoid placing herself between the class and the worship center.

    2. *Projected materials.*
      a. *The motion picture.* Thomas Edison is usually given credit for having invented "movies." In 1889 he succeeded in using a strip of Eastman film in his kinetoscope, for which he was granted a patent in 1891. There were, however, a number of earlier experiments in both Europe and America. Because of contemporary experimenters and inventers, Edison launched law suits to protect his patented invention.

The first commercial use of the movie was on Broadway, New York City, in 1894. The first motion-picture theater was opened in Pittsburgh, Pennsylvania, in 1905. As the movie industry expanded, the film production became centralized in California. Hollywood came to be synonymous with moving pictures. The salaries of movie stars and box-office receipts have risen to astronomical heights. The movie theater became the standard place of amusement for children on Saturdays, for young people on dates,

---

[4] Flannelgraphs are sold under different trade names, pict-o-graph, dramagraph, gospel-graphs, suede-graphs, etc.

and for parents and grandparents wanting to relax. Within the past decade, however, television has come to threaten the very life of the movie theater. Throughout the land hundreds of movie theaters have had to close their doors. TV sets became as indispensable in the American home as the radio had been. Even the poorest cottages display TV antennae.

The movie created a problem within the Christian church. In conservative circles the movie theater was taboo. The very name "theater" suggested that it was evil. Conservative clergymen preached against Hollywood with vim and vigor. In order that they might more intelligently preach against the evil, some of these clergymen attended a few of these nefarious performances in distant cities, where they would not be seen by their church members. Young people were warned of the danger, and children from Christian homes were forbidden to see such pictures. Objective studies made by psychologists and sociologists revealed the danger to children's minds caused by most of these films.[5]

The more liberal churches saw in the movie a device for bringing people into church on Sunday evening. The seats were free, and many of the same films were shown in the church as were shown in the movie theater. But the church was not able to compete with the movies in the matter of recruiting people on a Sunday night and soon abandoned the movie as a bait for church attendance.

Missionaries returning from the foreign field brought pictures that could be transferred to slides and shown on the screen. Some conservative churches permitted the use of missionary pictures if they were on slides, but forbade them if they were on a film. As long as the picture stood still it was acceptable, but if it moved it was dangerous. Some churches modified the bylaws of their constitution so as to bar movies. In other churches the pictures might be shown in a private home, a schoolhouse, or a hall, but not in the sanctuary of the church.

In 1897 a three-reel picture of the "Passion Play" was made in New York. Several years later "The King of Kings" was produced. It was C. O. Baptista, however, who made the movie acceptable to evangelical churches. Using only converted persons, he produced religious films which, though at first amateurish and far from professional in quality, became very popular. Reports of conversions as a result of their showing caused evangelistic, conservative

---

[5] Eastman, *Our Movie-Made Children.*

churches to look upon the use of certain films without serious objection, and often with favor.

James K. Friedrich, a Protestant Episcopal clergyman, used an inheritance of one hundred thousand dollars from his father in the founding of a corporation for producing religious motion pictures. In 1938 he organized Cathedral Films. A number of other producers of religious films have come into being both in America and in Europe. These films may be purchased or rented; rental bureaus and libraries are found in most of our larger cities. In recent years a film on Martin Luther has been made and released. One on John Wesley, the father of Methodism, has also been made.

Now that the objections to the use of moving pictures have largely been removed, and their use sanctioned, there is danger of their too frequent use. Then, too, there is now available a confusing number of films. When a program committee does not know what to plan, someone hits upon the bright idea of suggesting a film; so a film it is, whether it contributes educationally or not. Films should be carefully selected as to the age of the group for which they are to be used and as to the objective of their use. The equipment should be set up and tested in advance, and the film to be used should be previewed. The group should be prepared for the presentation, and after the showing there should be an evaluation.

b. *The film strip.* For educational purposes the film strip is often more effective than the moving picture. The film strip is made up of selected frames from films used for movies. These frames may be held in focus on the screen for several minutes, as the leader or teacher interprets. They are inexpensive to rent or purchase, and the projectors used are not expensive.

c. *Slides.* Slides have the advantage over the film and film strip in that they may be rearranged. The order of showing may be changed, certain slides may be omitted and others added. The Kodochrome 2 x 2 have largely supplanted the older 3¼ x 4 glass mounts. A slide projector and portable screen do not require the investment of a large sum of money. Film-strip adapters may be secured at a slight additional cost.

d. *Opaque projector.* The old-type magic lantern was an opaque projector, but a new type of opaque projector is now on the market. Photographs, pictures from pages of books and periodicals, diagrams, charts, maps, and so forth may be shown on the screen without first making transparent slides. Because of the cost and their limited use in Christian education, these opaque projectors have as yet not become popular outside of college and university classrooms.

VI. *Supplementary Methods.*

1. *Phonograph records.* Children's Bible stories and other fascinating stories as well as songs are now available in record form. These may be used at home or in the class. They may be used as a musical background for silent movies, film strips, or slides.

2. *Tape recorders.* A recent arrival in the field of Christian education is the tape recorder. Children's Christmas programs may be recorded and then reproduced in the home of some sick child or an adult invalid. A teacher may improve his teaching techniques by having a half-hour teaching session recorded and later reproduced, and the teaching evaluated by himself and his colleagues. Likewise a worship program may be recorded and evaluated at a teacher's meeting.

3. *Television.* Television is still in its swaddling clothes. It is as yet too early to predict what contribution it will make to Christian education of the future. As the morning devotions on the radio programs have influenced our American homes, we may anticipate that TV with its vision as well as voice may influence even more. A televised morning-devotion with a family around the breakfast table, or evening prayers with a typical American family may open up new avenues of guidance in Christian nurture in the home.

4. *Recreation.* Another area where techniques of Christian education are needed is in the field of recreation. Learning takes place not only in the classroom but on the playground as well. How may games and athletics come under the influence of Christian education? How may the spirit of Christ be brought into the social activities of our youth?

The task of Christian education is challenging, but the techniques are confusingly many. As leaders we need to be oriented, to know where we are and in what direction we are to move.

REVIEW QUESTIONS

1. What is teaching?
2. What four questions did Betts propose?
3. What outcomes did he suggest?
4. Who were the world's greatest teachers according to Wilds?
5. What five factors determine the choice of teaching methods?
6. What is motivation?
7. What are the seven principles of good storytelling?
8. How may the dramatic method of teaching be used?
9. Name three children's Bible-story books.

10. For what age group is the lecture method best suited?
11. What is *recitation?*
12. What are some of the problems in using socialized recitation?
13. What is a *social project?*
14. What are *manual-arts* projects?
15. Name five nonprojected teaching aids.
16. What is the purpose of a flannelgraph?
17. Who invented motion pictures?
18. Name two films of a religious nature produced early in the history of the movies.
19. Who was C. O. Baptista?
20. Who was James K. Friedrich?
21. What two Protestant leaders are being presented in modern films?
22. What are film strips?
23. What are the advantages of the slides in teaching?
24. What was the forerunner of the modern opaque projector?
25. How may phonograph records be used in Christian education?

QUESTIONS FOR DISCUSSION

1. What is pedagogy?
2. Some good teachers have never taken a course in how to teach, while some poor teachers have taken several. Explain.
3. When may methods become a hindrance in teaching?
4. What is the value of being familiar with several methods of teaching?
5. What methods were used by the Sunday-school teachers who instructed you?
6. What would your comments now be about the methods they used?
7. What equipment is necessary for the use of manual arts?
8. Under what circumstances would you use a flannelgraph?
9. Indicate the selection of a film for a certain age group; give reasons for your selection.
10. If a thousand dollars were donated to your church for audio-visual instruction, how would you invest it?

Christian Education of Children

STUDY OUTLINE

I. *The Challenge.*

Irene Smith Caldwell introduces her stimulating book *Our Concern Is Children*[1] with the dramatic statement: "Yesterday a stupendous thing happened! Nearly six thousand unspoiled babies were born in the United States alone."

That babies are born is not news; that has been a daily event since the dawn of human history. But that yesterday there were six thousand of these neonates in the United States is startling. The same thing will happen today, tomorrow, and the day after tomorrow. Six thousand daily! Fortunately these squalling babies are not confined to one nursery, no matter how large, nor to any particular city. They are distributed throughout our entire country. Some of these new arrivals opened their eyes in modern hospitals, others in tenement houses. Some will grow up in palatial homes,

---

[1] p. 84.

others in slums. Some will be confined to the cramped quarters of urban apartments, without even a yard in which to play, while others will have the freedom of large farmhouses with expansive pastures and woods for a playground. Some will find their homes in parsonages, surrounded by a daily Christian atmosphere, others will be housed with pagan parents whose only reference to matters religious will be in the form of oaths.

Although infant mortality has through the advance of medical science been greatly reduced, not all of those six thousand babies born yesterday will survive and grow up to become mature men and women. But the future citizens of our country will be made up of those who are among the six thousand infants born yesterday. As our attention is focused on these neonates, we recall the questions of the neighbors of Zacharias and Elizabeth concerning their son John, "What then shall this child be?" (Luke 1:66).

Some boy may grow up to occupy the president's chair, while another (God forbid) the electric chair. One girl may grow up to become the charming mother of a Christian home, while another becomes a woman of the streets. What determines their destiny? Who is responsible for what they become? Are these children like sealed, stamped, and addressed envelopes in a local post-office, waiting to be delivered to the right address; or are they like blank sheets of writing paper and unaddressed envelopes, the letter to be written and the envelope addressed? Perhaps neither of these analogies are applicable. On the one hand the child is not a sealed container, the contents of which cannot be modified, and on the other hand the child is not a *tabula rasa*. Three factors are involved: 1. *Heredity,* which is sealed even before birth; 2. *Environment,* which is constantly in the process of change; 3. *Ego,* the individual's will to do or not to do.

II. *Heredity.*

The science of genetics has stated in scientific terms the thought expressed poetically by Oliver Wendell Holmes: "We are omnibuses in which our ancestors ride."[2] When the reproductive cells unite to initiate a new being, the heredity of that individual is sealed. Through the lineage of both parents we have received through the genes, the carriers of heredity, a legacy from our ancestors. Whether we like our inheritance or not, it is ours through

---

[2] The original quotation taken from *The Guardian Angel* is: "The body in which we journey across the isthmus between the two oceans is not a private carriage, but an omnibus."

the process of heredity. We cannot exchange our heredity for one we might prefer; it is ours *for keeps*. We may, however, exercise some control over the heredity of future generations, our grand-children and their children. The selection of a mate for life should be of grave concern, since the heredity of the next generation and generations to follow are influenced by it. The choice of a husband or wife requires more serious consideration than is found in moon-light and a romantic mood.

III. *Environment.*

The environment consists of the surroundings in which we live. What the soil is to the seed, the environment is to the individual. A gardener may purchase and plant the very best seed, but if the soil is poor, the crop will also be poor. We cannot change our own heredity nor that of the children we teach, but we can modify and shape the environment. A good environment may contribute to the overcoming of poor heredity, while a bad environment may hinder the development of a good heredity.

Environment includes a confusing number of factors; we shall consider the four that contribute most to the growth and develop-ment of the child: 1. the home, 2. the school, 3. the church, 4. the community.

1. *The home.* By home we mean the place where the family lives, whether that be a palatial city-home or a small cabin in the forest. The family is a social and biological unit consisting of a mother, a father, and a child, or children. The often referred to *Bethany* home of the New Testament would not technically qualify as a family, for the residents consisted of a bachelor brother, Lazarus, and two unmarried sisters, Mary and Martha (John 11:1).[3]

The childhood home of Jesus consisted of a family unit. Joseph, the head of the family, was a workingman, a carpenter (Matt. 13:55). Mary, the mother, is referred to in the gospels on several occasions (Matt. 1:18; 2:11; John 2:1; Mark 3:32; Matt. 13:55; John 19:25). The last reference is in the book of Acts, where she is included with the group of believers who met in the Upper Room in Jerusalem (Acts 1:14). Besides Jesus, there were four other sons in the family, James, Joses, Judas, and Simeon, and at least two sisters (Matt. 13:55, 56). Thus there were at least nine members in that family.

It was in this Nazareth home, surrounded by brothers and sisters, that Jesus grew up. Since He is referred to not only as the son of

---

[3] Some Bible scholars believe that Martha may have been a widow, her husband being Simon the leper.

a carpenter, but as a carpenter, it is believed that upon Joseph's death Jesus took over the work in the carpenter shop (Mark 6:3).

Paul, although generally regarded as not married, had much to say about the family and the home (I Cor. 9:5). As a child he had been a member of a home, and there is a reference to one member of his family, a sister (Acts 23:16). In his travels as a missionary he had occasion to visit many homes and make his observations. In Colossians and Ephesians he gives advice to both parents and children (Eph. 5:22; 6:14; Col. 3:18–25).

The family is the oldest institution on the face of the earth. It is older than Christianity, for Jesus, the founder of Christianity, grew up in a family. It antedates the State, for family life is found among primitive people who have no formally organized government. It is more ancient than the human race, for we find the family unit among animals and birds. The dens of the wild beasts and the nests of the birds constitute their homes where they rear their families. The pattern of family life differs, but the basic principle of the family as a biological and social unit is evident. It is the Creator's design (Gen. 1:27, 28; 2:20–24).

The family has the advantage over other educational institutions in the matter of primacy. It has the first opportunity to minister to the child. Before the child enters the kindergarten of the public school, the home has had complete freedom to instruct and to guide the development of the future citizen. It can shape the child's habits and attitudes pretty much as it pleases. If the home is negligent as to the full use of these opportunities before the child enters school, it can never regain what it has lost. As soon as the child enters the public school, the home finds that it has a competitor. The home no longer has the full control of the child's time and activities. The parents who resign the directing of the child's personality development to the public school are making a serious mistake. The public school is designed to help the parents in this educational process, not to usurp their place. The home and the school must work as partners in the task of training our children into becoming useful citizens. The home lays the foundation upon which both parents and teachers build the superstructure, a personality and character.

The Christian church is a family of families. The cells within that macrocosm are the microcosms, the individual families, with their individual members. Much has been said and written about the Christian family. It is the very foundation of our nation. The disintegration of the American family has caused grave concern to sociologists, psychologists, statesmen, and church leaders. But what

constitutes a *Christian* home or family? There is no particular
architecture that would characterize a house as being a Christian
home. There are no posted signs to announce, "Here lives a
Christian family." How could a door-to-door salesman know
whether or not the home he has entered is Christian? Roman Catholic families display religious symbols of different types; there is
always the crucifix in a conspicuous place. But what about Protestant homes? What external evidences are to be found? However, external evidences may not be indicative of the internal spirit of the
home. It takes more than a large family Bible on a table or a
picture of Christ on the wall to make a home truly Christian.
The Christian home can perhaps best be expressed in three words:
atmosphere; attitude; activities.

a. *Atmosphere.* Atmosphere means more than the air we breathe;
it is the spirit of the immediate environment. This includes the
pictures on the walls, the books, periodicals, and newspapers, the
sheet music and the song books on the piano. The atmosphere of
a home provides the stimulus to which the members of the family
respond. It builds itself into memories that will long linger with
the child, even after he has grown up and left the childhood home.
The atmosphere of a Christian home is an indescribable something
that one feels without being able to analyze. It is an experience in
the realm of the emotions. The familiar song "Home, Sweet Home,"
expresses sentiment rather than a description. It creates a mood
rather than an image. The Christian atmosphere of a home is
something intangible, it is a blending of so many different factors,
it is a composite. Even small children can sense it long before they
are aware of what it is.

b. *Attitudes.* An attitude is an opinion, a feeling about something. We have favorable or unfavorable feelings towards persons,
places, and things. Reverence, honesty, and kindness are attitudes.
These inner feelings are expressed in external ways. Attitudes,
like charity, begin at home. The ethics of children are largely determined by the attitudes of parents and other members of the
family. It is not so much what is said in the home as what is
praticed that tends to shape the attitudes. It is the family sense of
values that becomes the foundation for the child's moral life. Criticism of the pastor, church members, and church workers expressed
in the presence of the children leave indelible impressions on youthful minds. In this way the confidence of children in the church and
its ministry becomes undermined. Children are not mentally mature
enough to appreciate the value of constructive criticism. *Small*
kettles have big ears, and they have emotional content as well.

c. *Activities.* The home does not have scheduled activities as does a public school, yet there are certain activities that are of daily occurrence and tend to form a pattern. There are the mealtimes and bedtimes. Both of these offer opportunities for Christian instruction. There are the mealtime prayers, shared in by all who share the meal. Even very young children may make their contributions through offering brief memorized prayers. The bedtime devotions are sacred moments when the mother may help to create a God awareness in the minds of her children. There may be a story read from an interesting book, a story from the Bible told in words the child can understand, and the prayers asking for forgiveness for sins committed during the day and a request for divine protection during the dark hours of the night. What better preparation could there be for a night of rest and sweet childish dreams?

The observance of special days offers another opportunity for Christian education. Each week there is a special day, Sunday. Is that a day children look forward to with anticipation, or are the activities of the children restricted to the extent that Sunday becomes a day to be dreaded? Thanksgiving Day, Christmas, and Easter are family-centered holidays. Family traditions are built up and preserved. Each member of the family has a birthday once a year. How are these events celebrated? Do they have any religious significance, or is it merely a party with ice cream, candy, cake, candles and presents?

How are discipline problems handled in the family? Are they dealt with in a Christian spirit, or is the offender brought before the judge (father or mother) to be sentenced? Do children learn that disobedience brings discomfort, that the home is governed by standards of conduct? Does the home contribute to develop selfish, unrestrained personalities? The respect for law and order has its roots in the family and home.

2. *The school.* The influence of the school is second only to that of the home. When the child at six years of age enters the first-grade class of the public school, or a year earlier the kindergarten, he enters a new and different world. The children brought up in Christian homes have been carefully shielded from evil influences. The mother's eye has followed the child in his daily activities. But this maternal supervision ceases when the child enters school. She may escort her child to the school and the classroom, but there she must surrender her offspring to another woman, the teacher, who will take over the supervision and direction of the child's activities. To the sensitive mother this separation causes deep concern, not to say agony. It is not that she doesn't have confidence

in the program of the school nor have faith in the ability of the teacher, but the mother feels as though she is being dismissed from her place as the chief director of her own child's activities. The teacher plays the role of a foster mother from morning until late afternoon. The child's interests become divided between the home and the school, the loyalty divided between mother and teacher.

The child that has been nurtured in a wholesome home will retreat with relief to the familiar surroundings of the home after a day spent in school. He feels more secure at home than at school. The home can thus continue its influence upon the child. In fact, it is the home's last chance to make a vital impression upon the child, for when he enters adolescence and the high school with its manifold activities, the home becomes secondary in the life of the "becoming adult" child.

3. *The church.* Strange as it may seem, even Christian educators must place the church as third in the character development of the child. The reason is that the church has so few, though vital, contacts with the child. One hour Sunday-school sessions once a week do not afford opportunity for establishing character habits. The public school, on the contrary, ministers to the child five hours a day for five days of the week for forty weeks during the year. How long would it take a child to master the three R's in elementary education if he worked at it only one hour a week? Add to this the problem of untrained church-school teachers and inadequate equipment, and the situation becomes academically more acute. With these limitations, what may the church contribute?

First of all, we would mention the influence of the church upon parents in maintaining truly Christian homes. The spirit of the church could and should be cultivated in the home; thus the Sunday services would become occasions for ascertaining directions and stimulating motives. The ideals of the church would become realized in the daily life of the home. In the second place, the church should not surrender the social and recreational life of its youth to the public schools nor to commercialized agencies. Between-Sundays activities should be a part of the program of the church for its children. In the third place, the church should encourage its members to participate in the function of the public school. Why should Christian men and women not be members of school boards, of Parent-Teacher Associations, and be teachers in our public schools where a Christian influence could be wielded in the classrooms and in personal contact with the pupils? The curriculum does not include courses in religion, but religious ideals may be taught through example, even when not possible through direct precept. The church must not resign itself to a one day per week functioning; it must be active in one way or another seven days of the week with a special focus on Sunday.

4. *The community.* The community includes not only the home, the school, and the church, but much more. It is a wide circle that embraces the corner drug store, the ice-cream parlor, the movie theater, the pool hall, the tavern, the dance hall, the grocery store, the garage, the alleys, and the street corners. Learning takes place wherever children congregate, whether it be in school, on the playground, or on the street corner. The home may be ideal, the elementary public school the best in the state, the church may be evangelical and active, yet the community may wield an influence that hampers or even counteracts the influence wielded by the other three. Pastors, pedagogues, and parents need to recognize that they have a co-operative responsibility far too great for the church, school, or home to attempt alone.

Our communities need to be purged from organized social activities that tend to undermine the morals of youth and weaken their character. Some of these are operating illegally, while others succeed in staying within the limits of the law but are nevertheless a detriment to a wholesome society. Communities as well as individuals need to become Christian. Morally, slum conditions exist even in the communities where the residents live in beautiful homes surrounded by verdant lawns and mechanical luxury.

IV. *The Christian Education Strategy.* Socialized medicine has its critics as well as its advocates. It does make us aware of the responsibility of society for the physical health of humanity in general. Our educational institutions are much concerned with the mental health of children. Courses are offered and clinics are conducted in the interest of mental hygiene. The modern church is aware of the importance of spiritual health, of spiritual hygiene. If our children are to grow up to become the kind of persons God intended them to be, the church must make full use of other agencies active in the welfare of childhood. In doing so, it should not consider itself an institution ministering merely to the sons and daughters of the members of the church. Its scope should be as broad as that of the public school. This will make necessary the close co-operation with other church groups within the community, as well as with secular social organizations. All children residing within the community should be the concern of the Christian church. Christian education includes much more than conducting Bible classes on Sunday. It means exposing the homes of the community to the gospel and spirit of Christ.

REVIEW QUESTIONS

1. What is genetics?
2. What did Oliver Wendell Holmes call heredity?
3. How may we change our heredity?
4. How may we direct the heredity of future generations?
5. What is environment?
6. Name four factors in the environment of a child.
7. Why was the Bethany home not a true family?
8. How large was the family in which Jesus grew up?
9. What three characteristics of the home determine its Christian character?
10. What is meant by the *atmosphere* of the home?
11. What is meant by the *attitude* in the home?
12. What is meant by the *activities* of the home?
13. In what way does the public-school teacher become the rival of the mother?
14. In what way may she be an assistant?
15. What three things can the church do to influence education?
16. Why is the church rated as third in influencing the child?
17. What is the community?
18. Why is it important in Christian education?
19. What can the church do to make a community Christian?
20. What assistance does it need?
21. When is a community Christian?
22. What is the goal of socialized medicine?
23. What is mental hygiene?
24. What is the scope of secular education?
25. How far should the church extend its program of Christian education?

QUESTIONS FOR DISCUSSION

1. How may the home modify heredity?
2. How may the church modify heredity?
3. What is lacking in the average American home to make it Christian?
4. How may family devotions be conducted in a modern urban home where on five days of the week the entire family is not assembled at any meal?
5. What objects in your childhood home do you consider as having had religious significance?
6. What books that you read as a child have left the deepest impressions in your mind?

7. In what way did your parents evidence an interest in the public school?
8. How may a Christian public-school teacher wield a Christian influence in the life of a child?
9. How did schoolmates influence you in the elementary public school?
10. To what extent should the church concern itself with civic affairs?

8

Christian Education of Youth

I. *The Problem.*

Ever since G. Stanley Hall (1904) published his historic two-volume book *Adolescence,* educators have devoted much concern to this age group. *Adolescence* and *teenage* have become heavily loaded words. The attention of manufacturers and merchants as well as educators has been called to these young people. They have come to think of themselves as though they were a new species of the human race to be fed, clothed, and educated in a special way. Clothes, coiffures and cuisine are all to be streamlined so as to appeal to the delicate tastes of this "special" class of humans. Even the church has been influenced. The gospel has been sugarcoated, *fun* has become the yardstick in evaluating the youth activities of the church. The adolescents must be entertained lest we lose them from the church. The more serious aspects of the Christian life must not be stressed, for the adolescents cannot understand and appreciate them. We must make religion a pleasant experience.

Dr. Hedley Dimock suggests that we declare a moratorium on

the word *adolescence,* since it has been so badly used. But the word is in our current vocabulary, and we cannot rid ourselves of it by means of a moratorium. Rather should we try to ascertain the facts about this age group and then treat them, not sentimentally, but intelligently.

II. *Adolescence.*

Adolescence means "the state of growing up." An adolescent is thus a normal human being who has left childhood but has not yet entered adulthood. He is wandering between the two. *Teenage* is a popular rather than a psychological term; as the word implies, it covers the period of teens, from thir*teen,* through nine*teen.*

The period of adolescence extends from the beginning of puberty to the attainment of adulthood. Most adolescent psychologists would accept the period as beginning at twelve years of age and continuing until twenty-five. But the age range is rather wide. The twelve-year-old is perhaps a seventh grader in the elementary school, while the twenty-four-year-old is doing his research for a doctor of philosophy degree. Traditionally adolescence has been divided into three groups: early adolescence (12–14), middle adolescence (15–17), and later adolescence (18–24). In the Sunday school we have classified them as Intermediates, Seniors, and Young People. More recent attempts at grouping have been made according to the public-school classification: Junior High, Senior High, and College.

We often hear about "the problems of adolescence." There is grave danger that we magnify these problems and make them so important that the slightest difficulty looms up as a problem. Let us not forget that there are problems of childhood and of old age as well. Adolescents should not become problem conscious to the extent that they feel that, in order to be a typical adolescent, one must have not only a problem but a whole nest of them. There are problems of adolescence, to be sure, and these problems should be solved intelligently. But it is well to remember that the roots of most such problems are deeply imbedded in preadolescent soil. In other words, the adolescent who struggles with serious problems does so largely because of what was done, or what was left undone, before he became an adolescent. With this in mind it is well to survey hastily the period of childhood.

III. *The Period before Adolescence.*

At birth the infant is a helpless bundle of unorganized possibilities. He has inherited certain patterns of development because he is a member of the human race, others because he is a member of some particular race, and still others because of certain peculiarities of his parents. Psychologists refer to the newborn as a *neonate;* the term *infant* is really a misnomer as commonly used, for the word means "one who does not speak," and the age at which children learn to speak varies. The term *baby* is usually applied to the child under one year of age.

What the child becomes as it grows up depends upon two factors— heredity and environment. To argue which is the most important is futile, for both are essential to development. As Christian educators we cannot change the heredity of the child, but we can modify its environment and thus direct its development.

The significance of the early training of the child can scarcely be overemphasized. The infant who is pampered by indulgent parents and granted every wish will find it difficult to make the necessary social adjustment in kindergarten and on the playground. Many adult Christians are selfish, self-centered, and autocratic, because as children they never learned to curb their own desires or yield to the will and interest of others. A child who has not learned to obey at home will find it difficult to adjust to a scouting program or the rules and regulations of a summer camp. Such children have problems in adolescence because of preadolescent habits.

The home and the church have supplemented the influence of the public school in developing the child from birth to adolescence. If we would reduce the problems of adolescence to a minimum, we will consciously do all that we can to give the preadolescent the right directions in life. We cannot hope to do in our teen-age work within the church what has been left undone by church and home during childhood. In our youth work we are constantly building on the foundation of childhood.

IV. *The Church and Youth.*

Henry Thomas Stock introduces his book *Church Work with Young People* with the statement, "American Protestantism is genuinely interested in young people."[1] The book was published in 1929; the statement is still true. But the problem is, How shall Protestantism express its interest? What shall we do? How shall we do it?

Two factors are important in helping us to formulate a plan or program. They are *needs* and *interests.* Having discovered these, we need to discover what agencies are available to implement our plan. The adolescent does not grow up in the church. Only a small

---

[1] p. 1.

fraction of his time is spent under the direct influence of the church. Nor does the child grow up in the home. During early childhood most of the child's time is spent in the home with the family, but when he comes to high school and college age he spends less and less time at home with the members of his immediate family. The welfare of our American youth thus becomes the joint responsibility of the home, the church, and the state. Each one of them has some contribution to make. These contributions must integrate, not contribute to confusion and conflicts.

1. *Youth needs.* Nevin C. Harner suggests that youth, between the ages of twelve and twenty-five, needs to make six discoveries of basic needs:[2]

1. They need to find God.
2. They need to find themselves.
3. They need to find a lifework.
4. They need to find a lifemate.
5. They need to find society and their relation to it.
6. They need to find the Christian society, the church, and their relation to it.

To this list of basic needs we would add but one: they need to find Jesus Christ as their personal Lord and Savior.

2. *Opportunities.* The young people need guidance, first in the discovery of these needs, and then in attaining that which meets these needs. It is a quest rather than an adult-controlled following of a prescribed pattern. But it is a quest that requires intelligent, patient direction. It is an opportunity for the Christian church to take the initiative. Stock proposes six opportunities afforded the church to contribute to this quest.[3]

1. To help young people understand the nature of religion and the meaning of Christianity.
2. To aid in facing the ethical and social problems of the immediate present and the far future.
3. To create an intelligent and active loyalty to Christian ideals.
4. To help young people gain the power to do what they know to be right.
5. To assist young people in becoming intelligent world-citizens.
6. To promote opportunities in sharing significant service.

---

2 *Youth Work in the Church*, pp. 31–32.
3 *op cit.*, pp. 4–10.

Good as these six suggested opportunities are, they fall short of giving the chief opportunity of the church in dealing with youth—that of evangelism, the winning of youth for Christ and the church through a personal acceptance of Jesus Christ as Lord and Savior. The listed opportunities are good, but they are not good enough, for they fail to recognize the basic need of a Christ experience.

What agencies does the church have at its disposal that may be used in taking advantage of these opportunities to meet these basic needs? We may find that what we already have is sufficient, if and when effectively used, or we may find that some new agency needs to be devised.

a. *Sunday school.* We have, first of all, the Bible study in the regular Sunday-school classes. In many of the curricula for these adolescent-age classes we find a definite application of the teachings of the New Testament to modern problems of life. Intermediate, Senior, and Young People's Sunday-school classes have much to contribute. In small churches these classes may serve as social units for recreational purposes without organizing a separate society to promote the social life under church supervision.

b. *Confirmation class.* The Confirmation class is used effectively in several denominations. The meaning of *confirmation* is dependent upon denominational interpretation which varies. With some it is a confirmation of their childhood faith, while with others it is a class conducted by the pastor for his young people, totally divorced from the idea of church membership.

The age at which children are enrolled in the confirmation class varies from twelve to fourteen years of age. The length of the course, too, varies; in some churches it is a one-year course, in others it is two years. In some communities the traditional Saturday-forenoon classes have had to be abandoned because of Saturday work by the children. In some churches they meet on a school day, after school. In some instances it has become necessary for the pastor to conduct the class during the regular Sunday-school hour.

The curriculum is in general the same, Bible history and catechism. For the sake of interest, Bible history has been presented in a story form, using the Bible text itself only for collateral reading. In liturgical churches much is made of the confirmation act at the conclusion of the study course.

In many evangelical churches, the pastor, in addition to the regular instruction given, has a private interview with each member of the class. Those who give evidence of a vital faith in Christ are then recommended for church membership, but the entire confirmation class is not admitted as a unit.

c. *Scouting.* The program of the Boy and Girl Scouts sometimes interferes with the church-sponsored program for its youth. The opinion of pastors and church leaders in general varies with reference to the contribution of the scouting program. Some speak most highly of it, while others are critical. Where the church has control of the troop, by having as its leaders members from the local church, there seems to be a valuable contribution to what the church as such is endeavoring to do.

d. *Other organizations.* During the high-school years there develops a keen competition between the social and athletic program of the school and that of the youth program of the church. The schools are usurping more and more of the youth's time. If the church has nothing constructive to offer, it perhaps has no right to complain. The fact remains that children who have been faithful in Sunday school and church during the elementary-school period begin to lose interest and drop out after they come to high school. Shall the church plan and project a competing athletic program, or shall it co-operate with the school? The adolescent has only twenty-four hours a day, some of which must be invested in sleep, some in lesson preparation and class sessions, many in extra-curricular school activities; but a few of these hours should be spent in home and church. This is a situation in which state, church, and home must co-operate for the good of the future citizens and churchmen. The school has neither moral nor legal right to claim all of the adolescent's waking hours.

The question of church-sponsored athletics is not easily answered. Some churches have used athletics as a bait to get boys to enroll in Sunday-school classes. In order to play on the church team, one must be enrolled in and attend a specified number of Sunday-school sessions during the season. It is generally concluded that this is not a commendable plan. The classes should be made so interesting that boys will attend without using artificial bait. But the church should be actively interested in the recreational life of its youth. Young people are gregarious by nature, and, if the church fails to provide social opportunities, youth will find its recreational life some other place.

The wisdom of investing church funds in the erection of gymnasiums may be questioned. The attempts to plan buildings that may serve as gymnasiums, lecture halls, social centers, banquet rooms, and so forth, have as a rule not been too successful. There is too much money invested, and upkeep is too great for the limited use to which such structures may be put. There are the items of heating, light, and janitor services, besides the provision and replacement of necessary equipment. In a community where there is a YMCA, it seems the part of wisdom to engage its facilities for certain hours during the week when your own group may conduct their own games.

The church should, however, provide a youth room where the young people may meet for social events, business meetings, and so forth. If given the opportunity, the young people will be glad to furnish the room themselves. An artificial fireplace in a cozy room will provide an excellent meeting place for a small group of youth on a cold wintry night. It will help to make them feel at home in the church. In some churches there is a special Scout room, equipped and decorated in a way to gladden the heart of both the Scouts and their leader.

Although sponsored by the state and not by the church, the 4-H Clubs contribute much to the social, moral, and vocational development of youth. Its fourfold emphasis, the head, the heart, the hands, and health, is expressed in the pledge of membership:

> I pledge my head to clearer thinking,
> my heart to greater loyalty,
> my hands to larger service,
> my health to better living.

Their motto is: *To make the best better.*

The movement is conducted co-operatively by the United States department of agriculture and the state agricultural colleges. Under Christian leadership, the 4-H Clubs may supplement the work done by the church in rural areas. The movement is becoming quite popular in towns and cities as well.

e. *Youth fellowships.* Before 1800 there were a few sporadic attempts at organizing Christian youth. The nineteenth century fostered a number of such movements. We shall refer to a few of them briefly.

(1) *YMCA.* The Young Men's Christian Association was organized in 1844 in London by twelve young men representing four denominations. In 1851 it was brought to America.

(2) *YWCA.* The Young Women's Christian Association was started in England by Miss Emma Roberts and Lady Kinnaird. It was introduced in New York in 1858.

(3) *Cuyler's Association:* In 1867 Dr. Theodore Cuyler organized the young people of his church in Brooklyn into an association that had as its motto: *Young People for Young People.* There were four committees: Devotional, Visiting, Temperance, and Entertainment. This became the general pattern for young people's societies.

(4) *Christian Endeavor:* Rev. Francis E. Clark, pastor of a Congregational church in Portland, Maine, in 1881 organized a youth society, the purpose of which was to lead young people to Christ and into the church. The plan was to have weekly prayer meetings which all members would *endeavor* to attend. In their personal testimonies the members expressed their endeavors to live Christian lives, hence the name Christian Endeavor. There were three types of members: active, associate, and honorary. The phase of the work was threefold: *inward spiritual life, outward expression,* and a *dedication to the will of God.* Once a month a special reconsecration service was conducted. Although the movement began in a Congregational church, it soon became interdenominational in scope.

The larger denominations developed youth organizations of their own, The Luther League, The Baptist Young People's Union (BYPU), Epworth League (Methodist). Smaller denominations followed the example of the larger groups and established youth boards with youth programs. One of the most recent of these denominational organizations is the *Covenant Youth of America.*

V. *Problems.*

1. *Competition and rivalry.* At a time when the individual youth should be developing into an integrated personality he is subjected to disintegrating forces. The home, the school, and the church often become rivals for the high-school student's time and interests, rather than co-workers. The youth wants to be equally loyal to all three, but he finds that he cannot. The result is the disintegration of divided loyalties.

2. *Lack of leadership in the church.* If a youth organization is to be effective in developing personality and Christian character, it must have leadership. A dictatorship administered by the church and superimposed upon modern youth breeds resentment. On the other hand, youth activities without the proper Christian leadership may lead to results that are far from desirable. For high-school-age, church-sponsored organizations there should be tactful counselors representing the church. The real leadership, however, should come from within the membership of the organization. Our youth organizations should function as Christian democracies, not as military units subject to stern commands. A young married couple with Christian character and an understanding of youth make ideal counselors for high-school-age groups.

3. *Youth activities in the small church.* In large congregations there are usually enough adolescents to organize them according

to age levels. Thus there may be an organization for those 12 to 14 years of age, another for those 15 to 17 years of age, and still another for those who are 18 to 24. There may even at the 12 to 14 age level be a further classification as a boys' group and a girls' group. However, in the small church there may not be enough on any one of these three age levels to form a social unit.

This problem has been solved in some small churches in two ways, first, by grouping into two rather than three age groups. The high-school age constitutes one unit, while those beyond high-school age form the youth society reaching from beyond the twenty-four-year level to that of the thirty-year-olds. This makes it necessary to extend the range of the preadolescent group to include all those below high-school age. The other solution is to secure a director of youth work who can bring the different age levels together without a formal organization and adapt the program to the needs and interests of all concerned. This requires tact and insight on the part of the director. The important thing is not that we follow age patterns, but that we plan and implement a program of activities that produces the desired results.

4. *The exodus after high-school graduation.* In rural communities it is possible to conduct large Sunday schools and yet find the youth work reduced to a minimum, if functioning at all. It is not the fault of the local church, it is a matter of circumstances. Upon graduation from high school, many leave the home community to go to college. At the age when they should be most active in the local youth work, they are residing in other communities, coming home only at vacation time. Others go to the cities to find work. Our modern farms are mechanically operated, thus reducing the number of human units necessary to carry on the agricultural activities. Those who remain in the rural communities usually marry early and establish homes. With small children they do not feel free to engage in the usual activities of youth fellowships. In some communities this situation has practically eliminated the traditional young people's society. The youth work thus of necessity becomes focused on the high-school age, with the adult organizations lowering their age levels so as to include those who otherwise would constitute the young people's society.

VI. *Denominational Boards and Directors.*

Most denominations have boards or committees on youth work. But youth-work problems cannot be solved by boards and committees, but must be worked out in each local community. The denominational headquarters should serve as clearing houses for the experiments in the local situations. The task then becomes one of co-ordinating, rather than of directing. Attempts to superimpose a ready-made denominational program upon the local churches has in most instances not been successful. The present trend of using these denominational boards as clearing houses for the programs as they function in the local churches seems indicative of a more effective youth work in the future. The function of the national boards thus becomes that of counseling, rather than that of issuing commands.

REVIEW QUESTIONS

1. Who originated the scientific study of adolescence?
2. What was Hedley Dimock's suggestion?
3. What is the meaning of *teenage?*
4. What is the meaning of *adolescence?*
5. What are the three traditional age-groups of adolescence?
6. What is a *neonate?*
7. What is the original meaning of *infant?*
8. What, according to Harner, are the six basic needs of youth?
9. What does Stock propose as the six opportunities offered by the church?
10. How may the Sunday school contribute to the Christian education of youth?
11. What is the value of the confirmation course?
12. What may the Scouting program contribute?
13. What is the 4-H Club?
14. What are the objections to investing money in building and maintaining church gymnasiums?
15. What was the origin and objectives of the Christian Endeavor Society?
16. Name some denominationally sponsored youth organizations.
17. Mention four problems in youth work.
18. What three institutions compete for the adolescent's loyalty?
19. Why is it difficult to carry on senior young-people's work in rural communities?
20. What can the local church do about it?
21. What are the limitations of a national board of youth work?
22. What may it be able to do effectively?
23. What would you consider a local *experiment?*
24. With which of the listed youth organizations are you familiar through membership?
25. What youth organizations have not been mentioned?

QUESTIONS FOR DISCUSSION

1. What is the *Youth for Christ* movement, and what are its objectives?
2. At which age level in your adolescent development do you feel the church did most for you? At which age level did it do the least?
3. Who directs the youth work in your local church?
4. What pattern of grouping do you have?
5. What do you consider the functions of a denominational director of youth work?
6. What are the arguments for and against *open* and *closed* young-people's societies?
7. What are the advantages and disadvantages of interdenominational youth conferences (conventions)?
8. What is the value of denomination-wide youth conventions?
9. Should the board of youth work be elected by the denomination or by the national organization? Why?
10. By whom should the national director be salaried, by the denomination as a whole, or the youth to whom he ministers? Why?

Christian Education of Adults

STUDY OUTLINE

I. *What Is an Adult?*

An adult is one who has reached maturity. Achieving this maturity is not a matter of the number of years we have lived, but rather the sum total of our experiences as well as certain inherited patterns. For practical reasons we consider adulthood a matter of chronology. The traditional general classification used in the teaching ministry of the church is *childhood, youth, adulthood.* Childhood is considered to extend to about twelve years of age, youth from twelve to twenty-four, and adulthood from twenty-five and up. We recognize that the twenty-five-year-old has but little in common with the seventy-five-year-old, except that the latter may be a grandparent of the former. The younger person is at the glowing sunrise of life, the older person faces the sunset. Naturally their interests and needs are quite different. The half-century gulf in age is too great to be bridged by an educational device; hence, for practical reasons we must divide adulthood into three groups: *Young Adults* (25 to 34 years of age), Adults (35 to 64), *Aged Adults* (65 and up).

II. *The Young Adults* (25 to 34):

Young adults is a comparatively new term. It suggests that they are new at the experience of behaving as adults. J. Gordon Chamberlin suggests four groups within the general group of young adults: *married, single, college, noncollege.*[1] But two more groups should be added, *church members* and *nonchurch members* (professing Christians and non-Christians). To set up separate organizations to accommodate these six groupings would in the average church be unwise, but the leader of a group of young adults must have these differences in mind, even when they are organized into but one group.

Although church groups vary as to the age range of the young adults, the general practice is to include those between the ages of twenty-five and thirty-five, thus a ten-year span in age bracket. In a small church there will of necessity be but one group of young adults. For instructional purposes they will be in a Sunday-school Bible class; for social and recreational purposes they may also function as a unit. Young adults are youthful and active. They are interested in activity programs and are not satisfied with sitting idly by as spectators, watching others perform.

In a growing number of churches so-called "home-builders" groups are formed. Here young married couples may discuss the problems arising within the home and may formulate patterns for the ideal Christian home. An older couple may be chosen by the members of this club to serve as sponsors or counselors.

But what about those who are not married? They may still be candidates for matrimony, but have as yet not found their mates. The men may feel much at home in the fellowship of the older men of the church (brotherhoods), but the unmarried women find very little in common with the young married women who discuss their husbands, homes, and babies. They are scarcely edified or interested in learning how many teeth Mrs. Smith's baby has cut, or the food formula the pediatrician recommended for Mrs. Jones' Johnny. In a fairly large church the forming of a special group of unmarried working-girls of the young-adult age might be justified.

Young people who have gone to work rather than to college usually become *young adults* earlier than those who go to college.

---

[1] *The Church and Its Young Adults*, p. 18.

Often they have to assume individual responsibilities earlier than those who have been under college supervision.

Newlyweds who have formerly been regular attendants at the church services and active in the program of the church become so interested in one another and in the establishment of new homes that they come to neglect the church. Young men and women who are transferred to other cities by the firms for which they work often lose contact with their home church and fail to make connections with some church in their new environment.

The young men returning from military service constitute another problem for the church. From the experiences of the world wars we have learned that restoring these young adults to the church and the community is a spiritual as well as psychological problem. They are adults, but they need wise guidance in order to make the necessary adjustments.

Ralph Sockman calls young adulthood the dangerous age. We work with the children, instructing them both at home and at church in the teachings of the Bible. We prepare recreation for them under Christian supervision during their high-school years; we choose a Christian college for their further education; then, after twenty-five, they are on their own. In some instances we have perhaps been guilty of too much guidance, so that they have not learned to make wise decisions for themselves. We lose them from the church at a time when they have energy that is sorely needed in the work of the church.

If the Christian church is to retain its young adults as they emerge from youth, it must always be alert to the needs and interests of that age group. Society is teenage-conscious, and everything seems to be done both by the church and other agencies to cater to the teenagers. In doing so we cannot afford to neglect the young adults, who not long ago were those much talked about teenagers. They are the very ones who should be recruited for work in the youth programs of our local churches. Their families should be cultivated by women's organizations of the church. The babies should be enrolled in the cradle roll of the Sunday school; the older children should become members of Sunday-school classes. We must do all in our power to win and retain young families.

III. *Adults* (35 to 64).

The upper-age limit for this group is placed at sixty-five for psychological rather than for physiological reasons. There is no special physiological change that takes place at sixty-five, as there is at the dawn of adolescence or at so-called middle age, 45 to 55. There are, however, psychological changes. There is a growing trend in industry towards compulsory retirement at sixty-five years of age. For forty years the workman has left the house at a certain hour in the morning and returned at a certain hour in the late afternoon or evening. It has become a habit. Then comes the sixty-fifth birthday, and his habits must be suddenly and radically changed. He is retired. At first he enjoys the extended vacation, but after a while he becomes restless. Pensions, savings, and investments may insure him a fairly comfortable living, but how will he spend the leisure time that is his?

The period of adulthood should be the most productive period of a person's life. Emotionally he is more stable than in youth. Experiences accumulated during the years have made him wiser. His physical strength may not be what it was when he was younger, but he has learned how to conserve it. Mentally he is more mature than earlier in life, his judgment is better, his insight into problems is more keen. These are the years when he wields an influence in the church and the community. He has arrived at the period of life for which he has during the previous years been preparing.

This is the family period. The average person is married and has a family and home by the time he has passed the young-adult stage. He now grows up with his family, he learns from his children as they do from him. It is educationally a reciprocal process. The children go to and through the elementary school, through high school and college. There are graduations, engagements, and weddings. The parent becomes a grandparent, a new status. Eventually the children leave the home of their birth and begin to establish homes of their own. Father and Mother are again alone, except for occasional visits by the children and their families. The change that takes place within the family may be a gradual process, but it is nevertheless a radical change.

Those who have not married by the time they are thirty-five are on the verge of becoming confirmed bachelors or spinsters. There are, however, many happy marriages after thirty-five. Unmarried men and women need not become eccentric nor social recluses. The ministry of the unmarried aunt and uncle in the lives of nieces and nephews has never been appreciated as it deserves. It is possible to retain a youthful spirit while growing old by keeping in vital touch with children and youth. The spirit of youth is highly contagious.

This period of adulthood is one of temptations as well as of opportunities. In the effort to provide social and economic security for coming years there is the temptation to engage in questionable, not to say shady, business transactions. A certain business deal may be legally safe, yet ethically questionable. The church and the cause of Christ are often forgotten when the returns from investments are counted. Sometimes men who have been active church-members and respected citizens of their communities suffer scandalous moral lapses as they approach middle age. They may go through a period of recklessness akin to that of early adolescence. There is need for divine grace to keep one's feet on the straight and narrow path.

Physiologically the period from 45 to 65 is that of cancer and heart diseases. Reckless living in one's youth begins to take its toll. The breaking-down process begins before fifty and continues with varying rapidity. Some grow old early, while others remain physically and mentally youthful for a long time. Heredity seems to be a determining factor. It is from this age group that we secure the most efficient and reliable workers in our churches. But they have as yet not attained their full spiritual stature. There is still room and need for spiritual culture and growth.

IV. *Aged Adults* (65 and up).

There are two factors that have recently brought the problem of aged adults into focus. The one is the increasing length of the life span. The other is the compulsory retirement age. What shall we do with and for people who continue to live long after they have been barred from active participation in the industrial life of the community?

In spite of the deaths ascribed to the prevalent cancer and heart ailments, there are a large number of individuals who not only achieve the biblical three-score years and ten but who become octogenarians, nonagenarians, and some even reach the century mark. Many of these retain their physical and mental vigor. The state has planned social security and old people's homes; industry has provided pension plans. It is not enough to provide food, clothing, shelter, and a decent funeral when they die. These old people should be given an opportunity to live normal lives, not merely to exist.

With advancing years the restraints of self-discipline become relaxed, and as a consequence certain personality peculiarities become more evident. Pet peeves may become fixations, favorite doctrines may become religious eccentricities. Old people usually find it difficult to accept change—it may be a new pastor, a new hymnal, a new order of worship, or a new church building. Religion is thought of in terms of "the good old days when we were young."

But there are those who grow old gracefully because they grow old in the grace of God. The personality mellows and ripens for the harvest of heaven. Christian character becomes beautiful. It is like autumn with its multicolored foliage just before the advent of winter with its chill and snow. There is no reason why the sunset of life should not be the most beautiful hour of the entire day of life. There are retired, silver-haired pastors who are an inspiration and encouragement to the young ministers of the gospel. They are like a benediction. Then, too, there are older laymen who have time and energy to devote to the cause of Christ.

The Christian church has been generous in its provision for Old People's Homes, but in many instances they have become but waiting rooms on the way to the mortuary. These old people are conscious of the fact that they have become a burden to society. The church must plan a twofold ministry of the aged adults—the one for them, the other by them. There are numerous instances of the aged who are physically unable to minister to their own needs. The church is responsible to do something for them. The trend towards the state's usurping the traditional social-welfare functions of the church is to be deplored. Jesus went about *doing good.* The church, besides teaching and preaching, must not neglect its social responsibilities.

But there are older people who are mentally and physically in good health in spite of their advancing years. Here is a source of potential energy that is going to waste. Why should the local church not make use of these talents? There are many services that an old person can render even better than a younger person. There is the visitation of other old people who are invalids, so called shut-ins. A visit by another older person reading the Scriptures, praying, and staying on for an unhurried friendly visit may do both the visitor and the visited much good. Industry is giving serious thought to conserving this energy of the retired and investing it in some profitable manner. The church, too, should be concerned.

V. *Organizations for Adults.*

1. *Missionary societies.* The church-sponsored adult organizations are usually open to a wide age range. There are missionary societies, ladies' organizations, and brotherhoods. The adult area of the local church often becomes overorganized. Several competing foreign-missions societies come into being. Interest in some particular field or some missionary is responsible for the forming of interest groups that may grow into definite organizations. The objective is foreign missions, but even in a Christian organization like the local church there is the danger of rivalry, each group try-

ing to recruit new members and solicit funds. The total missionary program of the local church may become confused through such misdirected group-rivalry. Wherever possible, it seems wise to unite all of the foreign missions societies into one integrated organization. In unity there is strength. A survey of the adult organizations of the local church may in many instances reveal a duplication of agencies.

2. *Ladies' aids.* On the American frontier the traditional ladies' aid society served a real purpose. It was an organization of women to aid the work of the church. The women raised money for the work of the church; they provided opportunity for worship; they met a social need. The new settlers lived on homesteads on the western prairies or in the woods. The men met and talked at work or at shopping centers. The women with their small children were isolated in their log cabins or homestead shacks. There were no radios, no telephones, no automobiles, and there was no rural free delivery of mail. Church services were held in private homes or schoolhouses, before chapels and churches were built. These were family affairs, all worshiping together without any attempt at age grouping.

The women met at regular intervals, usually monthly, for an all-day ladies' aid meeting. They sewed, knitted, and so forth. While they worked they talked. There were devotions to be sure, conducted by the pastor, if and when they had a pastor, otherwise by one of the women. Socially it was a great event for the otherwise isolated women. They were brought up to date on the latest community gossip. They exchanged baking recipes and prescriptions for the illnesses of their small children.

When the articles of clothing were finished, usually in the spring, a public auction was held. Shirts, aprons, and men's stockings were sold, with the proceeds going to the church. The ladies' aid societies survived, but became the sponsors of church bazaars and church dinners. In many instances the transition from the workshop to more modern methods has been done with a preservation of reverence and dignity consistent with a church organization. In other instances the change has resulted in a deterioration that has caused the church to resemble "a house of merchandise," if not "a den of thieves" (John 2:16; Matt. 21:13).

The women's societies still have a mission to perform. Far greater than the raising of funds is the contact with mothers of unchurched homes. Thus these societies serve as an agency in the church's program of evangelism. With the infants on the Sunday-school cradle roll, the older children enrolled in Sunday-school classes, and the mother affiliated with the women's organizations of the church, there is a possibility of winning the entire family for Christ and the church.

The women's society may become an effective agent in Christian education. The yearly program should include, besides Bible studies, a study of world-wide missions as well as the missionary interests and activities of the denomination. Altogether too often the missionary contacts are isolated experiences. A returned missionary is invited to speak at a meeting of the society. In the one-half hour at his disposal he can only give a glimpse of the missionary work. If the society had made a study of missions before and after the missionary's visit, the results would have been constructive and integrating rather than fragmentary.

3. *Brotherhoods.* The men's organizations of our Protestant churches, the brotherhoods, have perhaps developed an inferiority complex through being eclipsed by the elaborate and ambitious programs of the women's organizations. A church-sponsored organization of men is a valuable asset to the work of the local church. It is an agency through which the church may reach out and contact unchurched men in the community. It is an evangelistic opportunity. Then, too, the men of the church need to gather occasionally for social and recreational purposes. There are social, moral, and political issues that need to be freely discussed. The program of the brotherhood should not become a series of preaching services duplicating the regular church services. Picnics and socials may and should be sponsored by these brotherhoods.

There may be no need of setting an upper-age limit to membership in these organizations, but it seems advisable not to admit immature boys. On occasions they may be invited to attend special events. Brotherhoods usually sponsor father and son banquets. Often they give financial and supervisory assistance to boys' athletic programs, such as basketball, baseball, and so forth.

The men's organizations of the different churches of a community, town, or city, acting unitedly, can do much to curb social and moral evil and promote the good and worth while. Organized evil has a wholesome respect for the churches of a community when they present a united front. Legalized evil, operating in public dance halls, taverns, and similar dens of iniquity, may at least be kept within the limits of the law if and when church-sponsored civic organizations are on the alert. Organized pressure brought to bear upon lawmakers by adult church groups may and often does bring about changes in the law, curbing, even if not totally removing, organized social evil.

In the small church it may not be necessary to organize a separate brotherhood, since the men's Bible class may serve as the framework for both the Bible study and the social functions. It is well in all of these adult church-sponsored organizations to have a constitution that safeguards church control. Whether these adult organizations shall consist of an open or a closed membership is a matter that must be decided locally. There are advantages and disadvantages in both types. In the closed society you have a group of Christians banded together as a spiritual force. They are, however, limited in their outreach of evangelism. In the open society there are the *saved* and the *unsaved,* linked together in an organization sponsored by the church. These non-Christians may possess pleasing personalities and qualities of leadership and thus wield a stronger influence upon the group than do the Christians. On the other hand it affords an opportunity for bringing the *unsaved* under the influence of *saved* men. Whatever be the pattern of organization, the constitution should provide that the elected officers of the organization must be members of the local church. This will insure that the church has control and supervision of the program and activities.

4. *Sunday-school classes.* The American Sunday school is not for children exclusively; it recruits all ages. In almost every church we find one or more men's Bible classes. In some churches there are also classes for women, and in still other churches the adult Bible classes are for both men and women. The men's Bible class affords a fine opportunity for evangelism. Men who shy away from revival meetings and even from regular preaching services are willing to be exposed Sunday after Sunday to the gospel as presented in a class. Such a class also serves as an agent in Christian nurture. Converted men grow in spiritual stature as, Sunday by Sunday, they seriously study the Sacred Scriptures.

The apparent success or failure of a men's Bible class is largely dependent upon the choice of a teacher. Familiarity with the Bible is not enough; a pleasing personality is also essential. A Christian layman who is active in the life of the community may prove to be a better teacher for such a class than even the pastor of the church. The discussion method of teaching is recommended, but when the class is large it may become necessary for the teacher to employ the lecture method. In using the discussion method there is the danger that two or three monopolize the discussion, so that it becomes a theological debate instead of a profitable Bible study. Someone has said that in some of the adult Bible classes the need is for a referee rather than for a teacher.

There is a danger that the class centers around the person of the teacher, the Bible-class session becoming a substitute for the morning church service. Teachers with aggressive personalities but with strange ideas on religion may become guilty of perverting the hearers.

VI. *Studies in Senescence.*

The scientific study of old age has recently aroused keen interest. *Geriatrics,* the study of the diseases of the aged, has become of great importance because so many attain advanced years. *Gerontology,* a psychological and social study of old age, has been promoted by such books as *Salvaging Old Age* (1930) and *Sweeping the Cobwebs* (1933), by Martin and DeGrucy. The more recent books by G. L. Lawton have further stimulated interest, *New Goals for Old Age* (1943) and *Aging Successfully* (1946). To this list of books we may add *Older People and the Church* (1949), by Maves and Cederleaf, and *The Best is Yet to Be* (1951), by Paul B. Maves.

From the point of view of economy it may be cheaper to consign aged adults to old people's homes. Churches, lodges, the state, and other organized agencies provide such institutions to care for the aged. Psychologically the practice is seriously to be questioned. Going to such an institution is to many a personality-degrading experience. Much can and already has been done to improve the psychological as well as physical environment of such "homes."

Review Questions

1. What is an adult?
2. How is the teaching ministry divided as to general age groups?
3. What ages are included in the *young adults?*
4. What four divisions does Chamberlin suggest?
5. What two more need to be added?
6. What are the home-builders?
7. What does Ralph Sockman call the age of young adults?
8. What ages are included in the adults?
9. What diseases are common in middle age?
10. Why do we consider 65 as the age when one enters old age?
11. What are the problems of the many missionary societies?
12. How have the functions of the *Ladies' Aids* changed?
13. What are the objectives of *church brotherhoods?*
14. When may adult Sunday-school classes become problems?
15. What is *senescence?*
16. What is *geriatrics?*
17. What is *gerontology?*

18. Why are such studies important?
19. Mention some workers in these three fields.
20. What is the difference between a *home* and an *institution?*
21. Give an example of psychological improvement in care for the aged.
22. Give an example of physical improvement in care for the aged.
23. What are the limitations of pensions in providing for old age?
24. What has the church attempted to do for the aged?
25. What more could it do?

QUESTIONS FOR DISCUSSION

1. Why has the young adult become a forgotten person?
2. What is your church doing for this age group?
3. What are arguments for and against calling a pastor fifty years of age?
4. When do grandparents become a problem in Christian education?
5. What are some of the problems of retirement?
6. Interview some person over 70 years of age. Write up the interview.
7. What is an *endowment insurance policy?*
8. What is *Social Security,* and how does it provide for old age?
9. What is an *annuity policy,* and how does it provide for old age?
10. How are you planning for your old age?

The Sunday Church School

STUDY OUTLINE

I. *Definition.*

The most active agency in the teaching ministry of most churches in our day is the Sunday school. As the name suggests, it is a church-sponsored school that functions on Sunday. Some prefer to call it the Sunday Bible school, others the Sabbath school. The term most generally used is *Sunday school.* For the sake of consistency we shall follow the more recent trend of referring to it as the *Sunday church school.* We will in our studies consider three types of church-sponsored schools, the *Sunday church school,* the *daily vacation church school,* and the *weekday church school.* All three are schools that are sponsored by the church. They all have Christian objectives, but they differ as to the time of meeting.

II. *Forerunners of the Sunday School Movement.*

The modern Sunday school movement came into being as a noble experiment by an English journalist, Robert Raikes. Sensing a spiritual as well as social need, he began his experiment in Gloucester, England. There were a number of earlier sporadic attempts to gather children for religious instruction on Sunday, but they were isolated instances that did not give birth to a movement. There was one such attempt in Roxbury, Massachusetts, in 1665, another in Norwich, Connecticut, in 1674. Then, too, there were organizations for the promotion of the gospel that contributed to the Sunday school movement. In England the Society for the Promotion of Christian Knowledge was founded in 1698. A Swedish clergyman, C. G. Wrangel, under the influence of John Wesley, organized in Sweden the *Societas svecana pro fide et Christianisimo* (The Swedish Society for Faith and Christianity) in 1771. In 1777 this society began to establish schools in Stockholm for the religious instruction of persons over fifteen years of age who were lacking in religious knowledge. Younger children who were unable to attend school because of work in factories and shops were admitted to the classes, since these classes were usually held on Sunday. The teachers were young clergymen.

III. *The Birth of the Sunday School.*

1. *Robert Raikes.* Robert Raikes was born in Gloucester, England, September 14, 1735, and died April 5, 1811. He was a well-to-do journalist, and publisher of the *Gloucester Journal.* He was an aristocrat living in a beautiful home; he dressed in expensive clothes; in fact, he was considered by some as being vain. In some respects Raikes resembled the rich man in Jesus' parable of the Rich Man and Lazarus. But unlike the rich man in the parable, he did not forget the poor Lazarus at his door. He was much concerned with the lot of the unfortunate victims of society.

Social conditions in England in Raikes' day were deplorable. The rural population was largely illiterate, poorly housed, coarsely clothed, and hungry. In industrial cities like Gloucester conditions were even worse. There was vice and crime that the ruling class attempted to control by means of drastic laws and severe penalties. As a result, the prisons were full of people of all types, from hardened criminals to persons imprisoned because of their inability to pay their debts. Raikes took a special interest in these prisoners. He rendered aid in the form of food, clothing, and even money. But the work was discouraging, since not long after a prisoner had been released, he was usually back in prison again.

Raikes came to recognize that he was merely treating symptoms, the cause remaining untouched. At that time England had no system of public education, so that only the children of the upper classes were granted educational advantages. The majority of the children grew up illiterate and pagan. There were no labor laws, and even young children worked in the pin factories of Gloucester. On Sundays these young children were turned loose on the streets for a day of wicked freedom. There were churches, to be sure, but these were for adults. Robert Raikes was himself a member of the Anglican Church.

2. *Sophia Cooke.* Sophia Cooke experienced conversion at the age of eighteen and joined the Methodist Society. One Sunday Robert Raikes chanced to meet Miss Cooke in one of the slum areas of Gloucester. Seeing the streets filled with ragged urchins, foul mouthed as well as foul faced, he turned to Miss Cooke and exclaimed, "What shall we do with these poor neglected children?" Evidently Miss Cooke had given previous thought to the problem, for she replied, "Let us teach them to read and write and take them to church." [1]

Sophia Cooke later married a Methodist pastor, Samuel Bradburn, called the Demosthenes of Methodism. She died in 1834 at seventy-five years of age. The *Methodist Magazine* published a brief but informative obituary. Except for this obituary we know practically nothing about Sophia Cooke Bradburn. In memory of Robert Raikes there are two monuments, one in London, England, the other in Queen's Park, Toronto, Canada. Sophia Cooke is practically forgotten, yet it was she who planted an idea in the mind of Robert Raikes. This idea germinated and grew until it has become the world-wide Sunday school movement. There have been in the development of the Sunday school movement many such now forgotten personalities. The great lights in leadership have often received their inspiration and ideas from lesser lights. These unknown workers belong to the "cloud of witnesses" referred to by the author of the book of Hebrews (12:1).

3. *The first Sunday school.* The first Sunday school was started in 1780. It met in a kitchen 11 by 8 by 6½ feet. In the November 3, 1783, issue of his Journal, Raikes described his educational project as follows:

> The hour of assembly on Sunday mornings prescribed in our rules is eight o'clock . . . Twenty is the number allotted to each teacher, the sexes are kept separate. The twenty are divided into four classes; the children who show any superiority in attainment are placed as leaders of these small classes, and are employed in teaching the others their letters, or in hear-

---

[1] Addie Grace Wardle, *History of the Sunday School Movement in the Methodist Episcopal Church,* p. 17.

ing them read in a low whisper . . . Their attending the
service of the church once a day has, to me, seemed sufficient.[2]

It is interesting to note the early hour of meeting; later the hours
were set as 10 a.m. to 12 noon, then one hour for lunch, then from
1 p.m. to 3 p.m. back to school, from 3 p.m. to 4:30 p.m. in church,
from 4:30 p.m. to 5:30 p.m. in school again. The children were
then sent home with a warning not to play in the street. There
were separate classes for boys and girls, and the monitorial system
of instruction was used. The motto of the schools was "Clean hands,
clean faces, combed hair." The teachers were paid a shilling a
day. It is reported that the very first school attempted was a failure. Mrs. Meredith who lived in Sooty Alley, one of the worst slum
areas in the city, opened her kitchen to the class and became the
teacher; but the combined efforts of Mrs. Meredith and Mr. Raikes
with his cane could not control the boys, so the effort was abandoned.[3]

The first successful Sunday school was conducted in a Mrs. King's
kitchen with a Mrs. Critchely as a teacher. Mrs. King had been
manager of an inn near the county jail. Mr. King was one of the
teachers. Mr. Raikes helped in the work by telling Bible stories.
He took a particular interest in the boys he had befriended in jail.
As rewards for good work, Mr. Raikes gave combs, pennies, and New
Testaments. The age of the pupils ranged from six to fourteen. A
number of schools were started in the different slum areas of
Gloucester. One of the objectives was to keep the children off the
streets on Sundays; another objective was to teach them to read and
write; the third objective was to bring them the gospel.

John Wesley edited the *Arminian Magazine* in which, in the
January, 1785, issue, he printed an article written by Robert Raikes
under the caption, "An Account of the Sunday Charity Schools,
lately begun in various parts of England." What the Anglican
Church rebuffed, the Methodist Society welcomed. In 1784 Wesley
reports his first observation of a Sunday school. It was on Sunday,
July 18:

> I preached, morning and afternoon in Bingley church, but
> it would not near contain the congregation. Before service
> I stepped into the Sunday School, which contains two hun-
> dred and forty children, taught every Sunday by several mas-
> ters, and superintended by the curate. So many children in
> one parish are restrained from open sin, and taught a little

---

[2] *The Pioneer*, p. 70.
[3] Ralph D. Heim, *Leading a Sunday Church School*, p. 8.

good manners, at least, as well as to read the Bible. I find these schools springing up wherever I go. Perhaps God may have a deeper end therein than men are now aware of. Who knows but some of these schools may become nurseries for Christians.

In 1786 Wesley refers to having visited a school with five hundred and fifty children. In 1788 he attended a Sunday school rally numbering "between nine hundred and a thousand." In a letter written March 24, 1790, (the year before he died) Wesley commends one of his pastors: "I am glad you have set up a Sunday School at Newcastle. This is one of the best institutions which has been seen in Europe for some centuries, and will do more and more good, provided the teachers and inspectors do their duty. Nothing can prevent the success of this blessed work, but the neglect of the instruments. Therefore be sure to watch over them with all care, that they may not grow weary in well doing."

In 1785, "The Society for the Support and Encouragement of Sunday Schools in the Different Counties of England" was formed, subscriptions were taken, the queen herself heading the list.

The established church was not sympathetic to the movement. It had originated outside of the church and was promoted by laymen. The Archbishop of Canterbury called his bishops together in an effort to curb the entire movement, but the Sunday schools continued to spread throughout England.

4. *The Wesleyan Society.* Three Oxford men wielded a great influence in the Christian education of children: John Wesley (1703–1791), his brother Charles (1707–1788), and George Whitefield (1714–1770). John Wesley was sent to Georgia in 1735 to preach to settlers and Indians. In 1737 he taught the children of Savannah on Sundays. Upon his return to England he stressed gospel work among the children. In 1748 the Methodist conference passed a resolution pertaining to the place of children in their Society: "Let the preachers try by meeting them apart, giving them suitable exhortations." In 1776 Wesley commanded, "Wherever there are ten children in a Society, spend at least an hour with them twice a week. And do this, not in a dull, dry, formal manner, but in earnest with your might." To the objection, "But I have no gift for this," Wesley responded, "Gift or no gift, you are to do it, else you are not called to be a Methodist preacher. Do it as you can, 'til you can do it as you would. Pray earnestly for the gift, and use the means for it, particularly study the children's tracts."

From Wesley's Journals we glean the following:

> (Sunday, April 11, 1756)
> I met about a hundred children, who are catechized pub-
> licly twice a week. Thomas Welsh began this some months
> ago; and the fruit of it appears already. What a pity that
> all our preachers in every place have not the zeal and wisdom
> to follow his example.

> (Saturday, May 30, 1772)
> I met a company of the most lively children that I have seen
> for several years. One of them repeated her hymn with such
> propriety, that I did not observe one accent misplaced. Fair
> blossoms! And if they be duly attended, there may be good
> fruit.

5. *Sweden.* Per Palmquist, the Robert Raikes of Sweden, was
converted through the ministry of George Scott, a Methodist pastor
serving the English workers in Samuel Owen's factory in Stockholm. Per Palmquist, and his brothers John and Gustav, became
educators. In 1851 Gustav, later a leader among the Swedish Baptists in America, was leaving for the new world. John and Per
went with him as far as England. It was quite natural that Per
should call on his spiritual father, Scott.

Returning to Sweden, Per wrote an article in *Evangelisten* giving his favorable impression of the Methodist Sunday schools
he had visited in London. He reported that one school visited had
two hundred and fifty children enrolled and was taught by twenty
to thirty teachers, serving without salary. The children were boys
between the ages of five and sixteen. Securing permission to use his
own school building for Sunday school, Palmquist gathered twenty-
six children on Christmas Eve and told them about the Sunday
schools he had seen in England. The movement in Sweden thus
dates back to Christmas Eve, 1851. Palmquist, in addition to being
a teacher, was a publisher. He could thus print his own materials.
His work as publisher expanded until it became known throughout the land. He became a leader in the Baptist church in Sweden.

6. *America.* The first Sunday school founded in America that
survived was begun in 1785 in the home of a Methodist layman,
William Elliott. Addie Grace Wardle reports that in 1916 the
Sunday school completed one hundred and thirty-two years of continuous service.[4]

Of the many promoters in America, there is perhaps no one who
rendered greater sacrificial service than Stephen Paxson. He was

---

[4] *Op. cit.,* p. 47.

converted in a Sunday school to which his little daughter had invited him. It is reported that he organized twelve hundred schools with a total membership of over eighty-three thousand. His field was from the Alleghenies to the Rockies and from the Great Lakes to the Gulf. His salary is reported to have been a dollar a day.

On April 20, 1846, Paxson organized a self-managed, self-perpetuating, county Sunday school convention in Scott County, Illinois. The idea spread. H. Clay Trumbull of the *Sunday School Times* became county secretary of the Hartford County, Connecticut Convention in 1856. In the state-wide organization in Illinois we find such pioneers as B. F. Jacobs, Dwight L. Moody, and William Reynolds.

IV. *Sunday-School Movements.*

A merger of a number of Sunday school societies in 1824 resulted in *The American Sunday School Union.* In 1830 it was decided "that the union in reliance upon divine aid will within two years establish a Sunday School in every destitute place where it is practicable throughout the valley of the Mississippi." Through the effort of seventy-eight *dollar-a-day* missionaries, the union within the two years established 2,867 schools. For more than a century the American Sunday School Union has carried on its frontier work. It is nondenominational and surrenders its local work to some denomination when a local church is organized. It is thus a home mission project without denominational support or bias.

The Sunday school is now a world-wide movement. Thirteen world conventions have been held, the first in London, England, in 1889, when the total reported enrollment of teachers and pupils was 19,717,781; the most recent convention was held in Toronto, Canada, in 1950, when the combined enrollment of teachers and pupils had grown to 40,596,044, more than double that of the first.

V. *The Curricula.*

During the first century of the Sunday school's history there was no serious attempt at standardizing the curriculum. The Bible was the textbook, but the teachers made their own choice as to the sections studied and the verses memorized. This created what has come to be called the *Babel period* of curricula.

1. *Uniform lessons.* The feeling that a uniform series of Bible studies for the Sunday schools was needed led in 1872 to the adoption of the *International Uniform Lessons.* These were selected by an interdenominational committee consisting of five clergymen and five laymen.

The first lesson committee was given instructions by the association that had appointed them. These instructions were as follows. 1) Lessons were to alternate each year between the Old and New Testaments. 2) The lessons were to be chronological in order, beginning with the book of Genesis. 3) A part of each year was to be devoted to a study of the life of Christ, beginning with Matthew. 4) This was to be followed by a study of the work of the apostles and their teaching, as contained in the epistles. This first committee represented five denominations—Methodist, Baptist, Presbyterian, Episcopal, and Congregational. A seven-year lessons cycle was planned. The personnel on these committees changed from cycle to cycle.

Adjustments were made from time to time. To meet the demand for a denominational emphasis, the thirteenth Sunday in each quarter might be used as each denomination saw fit. Certain Sundays were reserved for emphasis on *temperance* and *missions*. Golden Texts and memory verses were added. Commentaries on the International Uniform Lessons came into being. In 1875 Peloubet's *Select Notes on the International Lessons* was published. Other such lesson commentaries are Tarbell's and Snowden's.

2. *Graded lessons.* When the uniform lessons were adopted in 1872, Doctor Edward Eggleston, editor of the *National Series,* voiced a strong objection. The problem of adopting the uniform lessons to the Beginners' Department led to the preparation in 1896 of separate lessons known as *Optional Primary Lessons. Bible Lessons for Little Beginners* came out in 1897. These latter became more popular than the *Optional* Lessons. The demand for a graded series of lessons increased until in 1908 when two systems were approved officially, the *International Uniform* and the *International Graded.*

The different denominations have proceeded to prepare their own graded lessons. One of the most dramatic ventures is that of the Presbyterian Church U.S.A. with its recent streamlined graded series.

In 1915 the lesson committee decided to issue a new series of uniform lessons termed *Improved Uniform Lessons.* These were released for use in 1918 and were to run in eight-year cycles. The lessons selected were to be adaptable to the different age groups. The second cycle covered but six years. The topics were: "Studies in the Christian Life"; "Some Great Christian Doctrines"; "Some Social Teachings of the Bible"; and "Some Great Men and Women of the Bible."

Without attempting to trace the development of these various curricula, it may suffice to state that the *Improved Uniform Lessons*

are still popular, especially in frontier and small schools, while the
graded series prepared by the different denominations are increasing in popularity. The major problem is not the materials but
the training of those who are to teach them.

VI. *Teacher Training.*

The average teacher is a volunteer, sometimes drafted into
service, but without training for the task to which he is called.
Conscious of the need for giving some training to Sunday school
teachers, the denominations have prepared and publicized training courses. These are usually of an elementary type and deal with
child psychology, methods of teaching, and organization. A demand
for content courses has led to the preparation of courses in Bible,
both historical and doctrinal studies. Some of these courses are
conducted on an interdenominational basis, others as local-church
projects.

VII. *Organization and Administration.*

1. *Organization.* The organizational pattern generally adopted
is as follows:

1. Cradle roll
2. Nursery—some include the cradle roll with the nursery
3. Kindergarten or beginners (4 and 5-year-olds)
4. Primary (6,7,8)
5. Juniors (9,10,11)
6. Intermediate (12,13,14)
7. Seniors (15,16,17)
8. Young People (18–24)
9. Adults (25 and up)

Some schools have a four-year *High School Department.* Very
small schools sometimes find it necessary to merge departments.
There is nothing sacred about the age groupings; they are merely
practical arrangements for pedagogical purposes. Large schools
often make use of yearly grading, each grade being in a separate
class, while smaller schools find the department or group-grading
arrangement more convenient. When there are enough pupils in
any department to form three classes, for example, the Juniors,
then the nine-year-olds may be in one class, the ten-year-olds in
another, and the eleven-year-olds in a third. In a department
where there are not enough pupils for three classes, the nine-, ten-,
and eleven-year-olds may be taught in the same class.

2. *Administration.* The Sunday school is directed by an elected
or appointed superintendent. Many local churches have boards or
committees that co-operate with the superintendent in planning

the work of the Sunday school. These boards are concerned with vacation Bible schools, week-day religious instruction, the Scouting program, and other youth activities of the church.

The assistant superintendent, as the title implies, assists the general superintendent. In the larger schools this may involve a great deal of time and energy. In the smaller schools he may serve as a teacher as well as assistant to the superintendent. Each department has a superintendent, and except for the very large schools this person may also serve as a teacher. For each class there is the teacher. The recruitment, training, and placement of church workers will be discussed in a later unit of this course.

The position of a secretary to the school is a far more important office than we sometimes realize. The keeping of accurate records is vital. No giddy high-school girl should be assigned to this task just to keep her in Sunday school. Statistics as to enrollment and attendance are meaningless unless they are based on accurate records. The files should contain a card for every pupil, on which should be recorded all vital information about the pupil and his family.

The treasurer of the school also holds an important position. Even small schools often handle fairly large sums of money. A bank account should be kept, and the treasurer's accounts audited annually. We are not only in the Lord's house, we are also in the Lord's business, and should therefore be both reverent and business-like. The Lord's money is to be handled intelligently.

VIII. *The Scope of the Sunday School.*

The Sunday school offers religious instruction to all ages from early infancy through adulthood. The Sunday school serves as the two arms of the church, the one embracing the children of the church to keep them from straying away, while the other arm extends beyond, into the parish, to reach individuals and families outside of the local church. At present the Sunday school is the greatest recruiting agency of the church. Both of its arms must be kept active.

REVIEW QUESTIONS

1. By what other names is the Sunday school known?
2. In what three countries do we find forerunners of the modern Sunday school?
3. Where was Robert Raikes born?
4. What was his vocation?
5. What was the social condition of that time?
6. How did Raikes show his interest in the social problem?

7. Who was Sophia Cooke?
8. How did she influence Raikes?
9. In whose home was the first successful school conducted?
10. What was the attitude of the state church towards the Sunday school?
11. What religious group befriended the movement?
12. Who brought the movement to England's neighbor, Sweden?
13. What is the *American Sunday School Union?*
14. When was it organized?
15. Who was Stephen Paxson?
16. When were the first *International Uniform Lessons* adopted?
17. Who strongly opposed them?
18. Why did the graded lessons come into being?
19. What denomination has recently launched an extensive program of graded lessons?
20. Why are teacher training courses necessary?
21. What are the departments of a well organized Sunday school?
22. What is meant by *yearly* versus *group* grading?
23. What are the administrative officers of a Sunday school?
24. To what ages does the modern Sunday school minister?
25. What is the analogy of the two arms of the local church?

QUESTIONS FOR DISCUSSION

1. Some have suggested that the teaching ministry of the church would be more effective if we dispensed with the *Sunday* school and directed our attention to *Saturday* classes in religion. What is your opinion?
2. What arguments are there in favor of uniform lessons in the Sunday school?
3. How should a church proceed in opening up a branch school in a new residential section?
4. Discuss the comparative values of buses bringing children to a church, or the church extending itself in the form of a branch school.
5. In which department of the Sunday school do you feel you received the greatest spiritual help as a pupil? Why?
6. Comment on the statement, "The church should include all of the expenses of the Sunday school in its annual budget."
7. When may the board of Christian education prove a valuable help to the superintendent?
8. Give arguments for or against the superintendent being appointed by this board rather than elected by the church.

9. What would you consider the duties of an assistant superintendent?
10. When may the superintendent become a hindrance rather than a help to the local pastor?

11

The Vacation Church School

STUDY OUTLINE

I. **Definition**
II. **Social and Religious Needs**
  1. The public school schedules
  2. The church class schedules
  3. The challenge of the vacation season
III. **Origin**
  1. Isolated attempts
  2. S u m m e r foreign-language schools
  3. Elk Mound, W i s c o n s i n, schools
  4. New York City schools
  5. The movement emerges
IV. **Organization and Administration**
  1. Local church
  2. Community
  3. Conference

V. **Scope and Effectiveness**
  1. Unchurched families
  2. Unchurched communities
VI. **Curriculum**
  1. Latham course
  2. International Council course
  3. Denominational courses
  4. Private publishers
VII. **Teachers**
  1. Students
  2. Housewives
  3. Traveling teams
VIII. **Finances**
  1. Annual budget
  2. Closing session offering
IX. **Problems**
  1. Summer migration
  2. Choice of curriculum
  3. Conserving results

I. *Definition.*

The vacation church school is a church-sponsored school providing Christian instruction for children during a part of the summer vacation. It is often referred to as the daily vacation Bible school (DVBS).

II. *The Need for Such Schools.*

The average American child between the ages of six and fourteen spends six hours a day, five days a week for from thirty-six to forty weeks a year in secular instruction provided by the state through the public school system. Thus for more than a thousand hours each year he is exposed to secular education. The teachers are, as a rule, well trained. The teaching materials and methods have been carefully selected. Attendance is required.

But the same child is not so fortunate when it comes to religious

141

instruction. One-half of our future adult citizens in this nominally Christian country are not receiving any formal religious instruction. Those who are enrolled in our Sunday schools at best receive but fifty hours of instruction annually. Attendance is not compulsory. The average attendance for the nation as a whole is very low. A large number of the teachers are inadequately prepared, and the equipment and classrooms are far from good. Meeting for one hour once a week means that the instruction is apt to become isolated from, rather than integrated with, the pupil's daily life. Lessons are not prepared by the pupils and, too often, are poorly prepared by the teacher.

In such a situation the vacation school provides an aid. The usual daily schedule provides three hours of instruction for five days, continuing through two weeks, thus thirty hours of directed Christian education is given. Since the average school continues for only two weeks, absences are few. The three-hour daily program makes it possible for teachers to use methods that the brief, half-hour Sunday school session does not afford. Some pastors and parents have declared that their children learn more in a two-week vacation school than in a whole year of Sunday school.

The summer vacation is a social and psychological problem. During the school year the children spend the greater part of each weekday in the public school rooms and on playgrounds. The teacher assumes the role of mother. Then comes the end of the school year when to the great relief of both pupils and teachers, but to the worry of the parents, the schools are closed and the children are turned loose. Unless this new-found freedom is invested in some wholesome activity, it may find its expression in mischief. In many cities there are supervised playgrounds; in others the children rush about on the streets to the annoyance of auto drivers and neighbors and at the risk of their own physical and moral lives.

The vacation school can render a real social as well as spiritual service. It usually opens the Monday after the closing of the public schools. The hours are usually 9 a.m. to 12 noon, thus following the pattern the children and parents are accustomed to. The afternoons are free. This two-week period serves as a link between public school and vacation. In some instances the vacation school is conducted at the close of the vacation season when the children are becoming bored with their vacation. It thus becomes a link between vacation and the opening of the public school fall term. In a few instances the vacation school is conducted on alternating days but continued for three weeks. The teachers, as well as pupils, thus have a day of rest between the days of school, which are Monday, Wednesday, Friday, with Tuesday and Thursday as days of rest. This plan has some things in its favor. Teachers like the free day for lesson preparation for the next day, pupils enjoy alternate days of freedom from classes.

III. *Origin and Development.*

1. *Forerunners.* Although the daily vacation church school movement, as we know it, originated in New York City in 1901, there were earlier attempts at sponsoring religious instruction for children during the summer vacation. There is a record of such a school being conducted in Boston in 1866, another in Montreal, Canada, in 1877. At Hopedale, Illinois, a vacation school was conducted in 1894, with forty pupils enrolled in four departments. The school was conducted by a Methodist pastor's wife, Mrs. D. G. Miles. There was an enrollment fee of one dollar per pupil. Each child was to bring a Bible; however, if anyone did not have a Bible, the school provided one through the American Bible Society.

2. *Summer parochial schools.* The summer parochial schools of certain denominations must be considered as contributing sources. The Lutheran and Reformed churches, together with other related groups, carried on such summer activities for a number of years. This was largely in immigrant churches ministering to people speaking a foreign language, Swedish, Norwegian, Danish, Dutch, and German. The Swedish immigrants may be used as an example. To the Swedish Colony on the Delaware, founded in 1638, the mother church in Sweden continued for over a century to send clergymen to conduct services in Swedish. Finally the descendants of the immigrants sent a request to Sweden that no more clergymen be sent to them from Sweden, since they could not understand the Swedish language—they were Americans. Many had married outside of the Swedish group.

The immigrants who arrived in the last quarter of the nineteenth century organized their own churches and worshiped in the language of their birth, rather than in that of their adopted land. Swedish was spoken in the homes, and Swedish papers, published in America, were read. The Sunday church services were conducted in Swedish, as were weddings and funerals. The courses in the theological seminaries were conducted in Swedish with but few exceptions.

Sunday school and confirmation classes used the Swedish Bible and catechism. The second generation must therefore learn to read as well as to speak the language of their foreign-born parents. Conversational Swedish was learned largely at home, as was also reading. Swedish day schools were recommended and attempted, but they never became popular. The problem was solved, at least temporarily, by the conducting of parochial summer schools. These became a combination of language and Bible schools. The teachers were either the pastors themselves, or often students from the theological seminary. Most of these were themselves immigrants. The local churches called them to teach summer school and to occupy the pulpit while the pastor was on his annual vacation.

These parochial summer schools flourished until the time of World War I, when conducting services in a foreign language became in many sections of the country forbidden by law. Germany was our military enemy. Swedish was a Germanic language, hence Swedish too was banned. The war thus closed all of these summer parochial schools. After the war many of the local Swedish churches dropped the name "Swedish," and services were for a time bilingual, usually Swedish in the forenoon and English in the evening. English hymns were added to the Swedish hymnals. Gradually, as the immigrant generation migrated to their celestial home and very few immigrants from Sweden came to take their place, the Swedish language gave way to the English. When the summer schools were restored, they became known as daily vacation church schools, conducted exclusively in the English.

3. *Congregational contributions.* H. S. Vaughan, a Congregational pastor of Elk Mound, Wisconsin, was much concerned about providing more training for his Sunday school teachers. In co-operation with Dr. William J. Mutch, professor at Ripon College, Ripon, Wisconsin, he prepared the plans for a summer school of teacher training which was launched in 1900. It was an educational camping-experience. Students came from far and near, pitched their tents, and combined camp life with teacher-training. These Elk Mound schools continued for a decade. In order to make the training as practical as possible, children were organized into classes for demonstration purposes. Gradually the instruction of the children became more significant than the training of the teachers. In 1908 the school was transferred to Ripon, Wisconsin. Although this type of school did not develop into a nation-wide movement, it is significant because of its high educational standards. Hazel Straight Stafford, who taught in these schools for ten years, states that *scores of successful schools were held.*[1]

4. *Baptist contributions.* Mrs. Eliza Hawes in co-operation with

---

[1] *The Vacation Religious Day School,* p. 10.

Howard Lee Jones, pastor of the Epiphany Baptist Church of New York City, in 1898 conducted a summer church school for children. She was superintendent of the Primary Department of the Sunday school of that church. The following two years similar schools were held. These attempts at using the vacation season for religious instruction were called to the attention of Robert G. Boville, superintendent of the Baptist City-Mission Society of New York. An idea dawned upon him. Why could not *idle children, idle churches,* and *idle teachers* be brought together into a number of such schools? The public schools were closed for the summer, so that there were countless numbers of idle boys and girls swarming on the streets of New York. Many of the churches were closed for the summer. College students and teachers were free to do what they pleased. Because of his administrative position, Boville was able to give the project the necessary promotion. In 1901 the New York City Baptist Mission Society promoted five schools, the next year ten, and, in 1903, seventeen.

5. *Interdenominational organization.* In 1910 the Home Missions Board of the Presbyterian Church U.S.A. adopted the vacation school plan, and in 1912 the movement was extended to Canada. In 1917 the International Association of Daily Vacation Bible Schools was organized. It was reorganized in 1921.

IV. *Organization and Administration.*

Most of the schools are sponsored by the local churches. They are then administered by the board of Christian education of the local church. A superintendent, who may also be a teacher, assumes the responsibility for directing the school. In towns and city suburbs the plan is often on a community basis. A governing board, consisting of representatives from the co-operating churches, co-ordinate the work and select both curriculum and staff.

In some instances the work is promoted by the denominational conference (geographical). Much pioneer Christian educational work has been implemented in this way. The American Sunday School Union makes much use of Daily Vacation Bible Schools.

V. *Scope and Effectiveness.*

A large number of unchurched families are contacted through these vacation schools. However, unless there is follow-up work, the net returns may be very meager. But many of these vacation-school pupils become candidates for the Sunday school.

As agencies for exploring new fields, vacation schools are most effective. Before entering a new field a careful survey should be made regarding interests. Attempting to plant a Protestant vacation school in a community that is more than ninety percent Roman Catholic would under most circumstances not prove successful. Starting a Sunday school in an altogether new field may prove so discouraging as to necessitate dropping the venture. This will cause embarrassment to the organization sponsoring the project. On the other hand, if a vacation school is used as an opening wedge, it naturally closes at the end of two weeks, whether it has been a success or a failure. If there is a keen interest in the vacation school, there is reason to believe that a Sunday school might be successful. The vacation school thus serves as a public-relations agency, paving the way for the further ministry of the church.

VI. *Curriculum.*

1. *Latham course.* Dr. A. L. Latham, pastor of the Third Presbyterian Church, Chester, Pennsylvania, prepared a course that for a number of years was popular in many churches. It was sometimes referred to as the *Chester Plan.* It consisted largely of Scripture memorization. It was a biblical-content course with almost all handwork omitted.

2. *The International Council course.* Within the International Council there was a committee on vacation schools. A series of associated graded lessons was prepared. Although pedagogically sound, these have not met the general adoption hoped for. The competition between independent publishing houses has led to nation-wide advertising. There is at present no field of religious curriculum construction where the competition is greater.

3. *Denominationally-produced courses.* A number of denominations prepare, publish, and promote their own materials. In order to appeal to other denominations the contents are usually theologically neutral. Controversial doctrines are generally carefully avoided. One denomination reports that more than half of its sales were from churches of other denominations.

4. *Private publishers.* Scripture Press, Gospel Light Press, and other publishing houses have prepared attractive courses for vacation Bible schools. These courses are largely biblical in content but make use of illustrative materials and pupil's notebooks.

5. *General pattern.* Vacation-school materials center largely around notebooks and various types of handwork. Considerable time is devoted to missionary studies, music, and worship. The theologically conservative courses build the workbook and handwork around biblical passages. In some of the more liberal circles the Bible is used only incidentally and then largely in the form of

dramatics. Most of the courses are planned for two weeks, five days a week, three hours a day.

VII. *The Staff.*

The teachers are largely recruited from theological seminaries, Christian colleges, and missionary training schools. Public school teachers often volunteer to devote a part of their summer vacation to this type of Christian education. Housewives with teaching experience render invaluable service in these summer schools. Since the classes are conducted in the forenoon, the mothers may devote their afternoons to the necessary household duties.

When the schools are sponsored by a conference, students are engaged for the entire summer season. The schools are staggered so that the team of teachers travel about like circuit riders. One team can thus conduct four or five two-week schools in one season.

VIII. *Finances.*

The vacation church school should be provided for in the annual budget of the local church. Where the schools are a community project, the local churches should anticipate their share and include it in the budget. If the schools are sponsored by a conference, it should make provision for them in its projected budget.

In some localities an enrollment fee is required, in others the pupils pay only for the materials. In other situations where the project is entirely home missions, no attempt is made to receive any contributions from the children. A generally accepted policy has been to invite parents and friends to the closing session of the school. The program consists largely of a demonstration of what has been learned during the course. The pupil's handwork is on display. Refreshments are served, and a social time follows. At these graduation exercises offerings are received for the support of the work. Psychologically this is a good policy, for parents may then feel that the school has not been on a charity basis. Whether their contribution has been great or small, the parents feel they have had a part in what has been done for their children.

The practice of depending upon this closing-day offering to remunerate the teachers is too haphazard to be continued. At best the wages paid vacation-school teachers is small, and it is scriptural that "the laborer is worthy of his hire" (Luke 10:7; I Tim. 5:18). These offerings should be supplementary to the budget, not a substitute for a budget.

IX. *Problems.*

1. *Migration to summer homes.* In the large cities a large number of families move out to their summer homes as soon as the public

school closes. The result is that many children are thereby deprived of the benefits of the vacation school. Rather than postpone the exodus until the close of the school, thoughtless parents either do not enroll their children, or they limit their attendance to only a few days.

2. *The choice of curriculum in community schools.* When several denominations are co-operating in a community school, the problem of the choice of curriculum sometimes becomes acute. With denominational bias it is difficult to be objective in the choice of materials. A curriculum committee representing all of the co-operating churches should study and evaluate several curricula. The attempt to select units from different curricula and integrate them into a course is rarely successful. Some communities rotate the denominational materials from year to year. The use of the Co-operative Curriculum is an attempt to provide for such community schools.[2] There is also the problem of what hymnal shall be used for worship, since each denomination has its own hymnals.

3. *Conserving results.* A two-week vacation school in a new field serves to arouse interest; much more is not accomplished. Children may be led to make personal commitments, but if there is no effort to follow up the vacation school, these commitments can mean but little. To have Christian instruction for two weeks each year, with fifty intervening weeks without spiritual nurture, is spiritual criminal negligence. The reports of spiritual victories won through the summer school are meaningless unless the Christian church is willing to water and tend the seed sown during the two weeks of teaching ministry. Spiritual neonates will starve and freeze to death unless spiritual nurture is provided. If it is impossible to start a Sunday school in such virgin areas, a field worker should make frequent calls during those fifty spiritually barren weeks. The Christian church needs to rethink its program of Christian education. The different agencies need to be integrated. The Sunday church school, the weekday church school, and the vacation church school are not independent kingdoms; they are rather like the states in our Union, all working together for a common cause.

REVIEW QUESTIONS

1. How many hours of instruction does the child receive in secular education each week?

---

[2] The Co-operative Publishing Association is an agency administered by the publishing houses with the counsel of the International Council.

2. How many hours of Christian education does the same child receive?
3. How many hours are provided in the vacation school?
4. What were the summer parochial schools?
5. What became of them?
6. Who was H. S. Vaughan?
7. Who was W. J. Mutch?
8. Who was Hazel Straight Stafford?
9. Who was Mrs. Eliza Hawes?
10. Who was Robert G. Boville?
11. What was his slogan for vacation schools?
12. When was the International Association of Daily Vacation Bible Schools organized?
13. How are vacation schools sponsored?
14. How are they directed?
15. What was the *Latham* course?
16. Name three sources of teaching materials.
17. What is the general pattern of the materials?
18. What is the usual length of the vacation school?
19. How are teachers recruited?
20. What is meant by a team of teachers?
21. How are finances secured?
22. What is meant by *vacation migration?*
23. How does this effect the work of the vacation schools?
24. What problem of curriculum does the community school face?
25. What is the major problem of conserving results?

Questions For Discussion

1. How would you meet the argument of some parents: "The children are so tired of school that summer school would be just too much for them; they need to be free from school"?
2. What do you feel the vacation church school contributed to your religious instruction?
3. What would be the advantages and disadvantages of having the vacation school at the close of the summer season?
4. If your community has a weekday church school, is it necessary to have a vacation school as well? Explain.
5. What arguments could be given in favor of conducting the summer school for four or even six weeks?
6. What methods of teaching may be used in the vacation school that would not be practical in the Sunday or weekday schools?

7. What would you consider a fair remuneration for a student serving as a vacation school teacher?
8. How would you proceed to promote a vacation school in your community?
9. What are the advantages and disadvantages of a community school?
10. What could be done to conserve the results of a vacation school in a new field?

12

The Weekday Church School

STUDY OUTLINE

I. *Definition.*

The weekday church school is sponsored by the church. It provides weekly a period of religious instruction to pupils in the public schools, during time when they are released from the regular program of the school. It is thus a co-operative project between the church and the state, the church taking the initiative.

II. *The Church and the State.*

The relationship of the individual to the state is not a new problem. Plato, in his *Republic,* discusses the issue. In the days of Samuel the prophet, when there was a change of government in Israel from a theocracy to a monarchy, the problem was brought into sharp focus. The prophet in no uncertain terms warned the children of Israel as to the demands of a king upon his subjects (I Sam. 8:10–18). Jesus was confronted with the matter when He was asked, "Is it lawful to give tribute unto Caesar, or not?" He did not answer by quoting from the Hebrew Scriptures, but by means of a coin. "Whose is this image and superscription?" The answer was expressed in one word, "Caesar's." Then Jesus uttered the oft quoted words, "Render therefore unto Caesar the things that are Caesar's; and unto God the things that are God's" (Matt. 22:15–22). The tempting questioners tried to trick Jesus into answering with an *either* or an *or*. He answered that it was *neither* one nor the other, but *both*.

These words of the Master have been interpreted to mean that the true Christian is a citizen of two kingdoms at the same time, the kingdom of God and a kingdom of man. But dual loyalties are extremely difficult. At another occasion, speaking about becoming enslaved by material things, Jesus declared, "No man can serve two masters: for either he will hate the one, and love the other; or he will hold to one, and despise the other" (Matt. 6:24).

There are some well-meaning Christians who claim that since their *citizenship is in heaven* they have no responsibility to any government by man. The Apostle Paul, however, seems to hold a different view. In his epistle to the Romans he declares: "Let every soul be in subjection to the higher powers: for there is no power but of God; and the powers that be are ordained of God. Therefore he that resisteth the power, withstandeth the ordinance of God: and they that withstand shall receive to themselves judgment" (Rom. 13:1–2). From the context it is quite evident that Paul had in mind the State, for he commands, "Render to all their dues; tribute to whom tribute is due; custom to whom custom; fear to whom fear; honor to whom honor" (Rom. 13:7). In writing to young Timothy he urges that "supplications, prayers, intercessions, thanksgivings, be made for all men; for the kings and all that are in high places" (I Tim. 2:1). On several occasions Paul made good use of his rights as a Roman citizen. Peter boldly declared, "We must obey God rather than men" (Acts 5:29). But the apostles were not anarchists; it was only as the state interfered with the dictates of their conscience that they protested. The early Christians held that if there was a conflict between the will of the state and the will of God, the latter was given the preference, even if it meant martyrdom.

In many European countries the church and the state are united. In England the Anglican Church is the state church. In Scotland it is the Presbyterian, in the Scandinavian countries it is the Lutheran. In the United States we permit and protect all creeds and faiths without recognizing any one of them as an official church.

The president of our country may be an Episcopalian, a Baptist, a Methodist, or a Presbyterian. Alfred E. Smith, presidential candidate in 1928, was a Roman Catholic. We have adopted the principle of the separation of church and state. The state is free, and the church is also free.

We sometimes hear the complaint that America is no longer "the land of the free and the home of the brave." When we observe the bondage of the subjects of totalitarian governments, we recognize that we are free. But freedom does not mean a license to do what one may please. Theoretically we are free, for the constitution of our country grants us that privilege; but in practice we may sometimes find it difficult to realize the freedom our constitution promises. The words of Jesus, "Render therefore unto Caesar the things that are Caesar's; and unto God the things that are God's," are as much applicable to twentieth-century Americans as they were to the Jews of Jesus' day. We are, however, often confused by not knowing what things belong to God and what to Caesar.

In the early history of our country, the church was very influential in the affairs of the state. When the Federal Constitutional Convention assembled in Philadelphia, in 1787, many of the states, as a part of their constitutions, had religious tests as qualifications for holding an office. Massachusetts required a belief in the Christian religion: "I believe in the Christian religion and have a firm persuasion of its truth." Georgia, New Hampshire, New Jersey, and North Carolina limited such religious belief to the Protestant religion. No Roman Catholic could hold a public office in these states. Delaware, North Carolina, and Pennsylvania required an acknowledgement that both the Old and New Testaments were given by inspiration. Pennsylvania added another, a belief in "one God, the creator and governor of the universe, the rewarder of good and the punisher of the wicked." Delaware stressed a trinitarian confession, "faith in God the Father, and in Jesus Christ his only Son, and in the Holy Ghost, one God blessed forever." Only one of the thirteen original states had never required a religious test for holding office, namely Rhode Island. Such creedal prerequisites for the holding of an office were scarcely consistent with religious freedom.

When the Federal Constitution was drawn up, Article 6, Section 3, was introduced: "No religious test shall ever be required as a qualification to any office or public trust under the United States." This, however, did not prevent individual states from setting up religious tests for offices *within the state.* In 1931 eight states still required a belief in a Supreme Being as a qualification for certain offices. Pennsylvania and Tennessee, in addition, exact a belief in "a future state of rewards and punishments."

The first amendment to the Federal Constitution assured religious freedom, nationally, for the future: "Congress shall make no law respecting an establishment of religion or prohibiting the free use thereof." Thus the principle of the separation of church and state was articulated. Theoretically, all formal religion is barred from the function of the state, but not from its practice. The president of the United States takes his oath of office *on the Bible,* a religious act. Congress is opened with prayer by a chaplain engaged by the state, again a religious function. During war, chaplains are recruited for religious service and are salaried by the state. These are only a few examples of the co-operation, rather than the separation, of church and state.

To whom does the child belong?

To whom does the child belong, to Caesar or to God? In theory we say *to God,* in practice *to Caesar.* In ancient Sparta the child was considered the property of the state. The parents were merely the servants of the state in the nurturing of the child up to a certain age, when the state took full control.[1] When the child was born, a committee representing the state determined whether the child was worth rearing or not. If it was deformed or sickly, it was done away with. Only the strongest and healthiest were permitted to live and grow up. At the age of seven, the sons were surrendered by their parents to the state, which trained them to become good soldiers. The Spartans accepted the philosophy that the child belonged to the state, and acted accordingly.

In Christian America we turn the child over to the state when he is five years of age. On the state-controlled educational assembly line the child moves from kindergarten, through the elementary grades, on to high school, then through college and university, emerging at the end of twenty years with his Ph.D. The state has provided classrooms, teachers, and curricula. The child has been exposed to materialism, hedonism, and a variety of other isms. The state assumes no responsibility for religious instruction, but leaves that to the church. This religious education is limited to an hour on Sundays, with wholly inadequate classroom facilities and with teachers who are sometimes quite indifferent to what happens to the child and who at other times may have a great deal of zeal but a minimum of knowledge. The average American home offers but

---

[1] Ellwood Cubberley, *The History of Education,* pp. 22–23.

little by way of religious instruction. The religious temperature is zero, if not below. Like visitors to an automobile factory, the parents stand by as they watch their offspring move along the state-controlled educational assembly line. They pay their taxes, and thus keep the line moving. When the child, now a young person, graduates from the state university, he is a product of the state; the home and church have been merely interested observers to the process.

III. *Parochial Schools.*

Parallel with the educational program of the state, there has developed a church-sponsored system of education. In this movement the Roman Catholic Church has taken the initiative. Maurice Sheehy, instructor in religion in the Catholic University of America, expresses the educational philosophy of his church in the following words: "The Catholic does not recognize as even half a loaf a system of education which relegates religion to an hour or two set apart each week." He continues by saying, "If the relation of the individual soul to God is paramount in life, education should aim at securing the Supreme Good, that is God, for the souls of those being educated, as well as the maximum welfare possible for human society on earth."

Though all Catholic children are not enrolled in the Catholic parochial schools, it is true that the church provides such education for those who desire it. The program includes the years from five through the college period. During those years, when we as Protestants relinquish our children to the control of the state, the good Catholic retains his children under the influence of his church. A religious philosophy of life is thus integrated with the secular instruction. In fact, the line of demarcation between secular and sacred is almost erased. A Catholic child may continue in Catholic education from his enrollment in the parochial school of his local church to his graduation as a Ph.D. from Notre Dame or any other Catholic University.

Among the Protestants, the Lutherans and Seventh Day Adventists have developed a system of parochial schools, and the Christian Reformed have developed a system of parent-controlled private schools. In 1949 four Lutheran Synods had an enrollment of 110,-282; the Adventists had 33,540.[2] In 1920 the Reformed group formed a National Union of Christian Schools which in 1949

---

[2] Frank E. Gaebelein, *Christian Education in a Democracy,* pp. 102–103.

numbered one hundred and thiry-three elementary and secondary schools with a total enrollment of 23,970.

Attempts have been made legally to curb these parochial schools. The most striking example is that of the Oregon case. In the autumn of 1922, the Oregon legislature passed a law known as *The Compulsory Education Act*.[3] Its wording is as follows:

> Any parent, guardian, or other person in the State of Oregon having control or charge or custody of a child under the age of sixteen and of the age of eight years or over at the commencement of a term of public school of the district in which said child resides, who shall fail or neglect or refuse to send such child to a public school for the period of time a public school shall be held during the current year in said district, shall be guilty of a misdemeanor and each day's failure to send such child to a public school shall constitute a separate offence; provided, that in the following cases, children shall not be required to attend public school: a) Children physically unable, b) Children who have completed the eighth grade, c) Distance from school, d) Private instruction.

The purpose of this law was to close all private and parochial schools. A test case was appealed to the United States Supreme Court, which gave as its opinion that the law was unconstitutional. The court pointed out that the private and church schools were "engaged in a kind of undertaking not inherently harmful, but long regarded as useful and meritorious." The court went on to say, "The child is not the mere creature of the state; those who nurture him and direct his destiny have the right, coupled with the high duty, to recognize and prepare him for additional obligations." Thus the United States Supreme Court has stated that the child does not belong to the state. The state is concerned that every child be given an adequate education, but it may not prescribe how and by whom.

Parochial schools are only a partial solution to our problem of giving our children adequate religious instruction. When it comes to Protestantism by and large, it is rather unlikely that the parochial system will ever take root.[4]

IV. *Bible Study for Credit.*

1. *North Dakota plan.* In North Dakota and Colorado plans for granting public school credit for religious education outside of the schools were launched. In North Dakota Vernon P. Squirers, pro-

---

[3] *Oregon Laws*, 1923, Chapter I, Section 5259.
[4] Frank E. Gaebelein, *op. cit.*, p. 103.

fessor at the state university, proposed a plan whereby credit might be given for Bible study. The plan was recommended by the State Educational Association, endorsed by the Conference of City Superintendents and High School Principals, and adopted by the State Board of Education *as a purely educational measure.* The only textbook was the Bible itself, and any version might be used. The state prepared the study syllabus (this was the responsibility of five members of the State Board of Education). The state would prepare the examinations. No public educational funds were to be used for promotion; all such expenses were to be born by the State Sunday School Association. The plan was adopted in 1912, and in January the following year the first examinations were given. Fifteen young people took the test, eleven passed the examination. In June of that year one hundred and twelve papers from thirty-two communities were submitted. Fourteen failed that test. One half unit towards the fifteen or sixteen units required for graduation from high school could be earned through the Bible study. The courses were taught in Sunday school classes, youth organizations, or through individual study. Although half a dozen states evidenced an active interest, the North Dakota plan of Bible study for high school credit did not develop into what could be called a movement.

2. *Colorado plan.* In September, 1910, D. D. Forward, a Baptist pastor in Greeley, Colorado, suggested to the authorities of the State Teachers' College located in that city that, if they would grant credit to their students, he would teach a Bible class in his own church. The offer was accepted, and in September the following year, two hundred and fifty students were enrolled in his course on the *Life of Jesus.* Sixty of these students were Roman Catholics.

The plan seemed so successful that it was suggested that it be extended to include credit in the high schools as well. The Educational Council of the State Teachers' Association appointed a committee of three to co-operate with a similar committee from the State Sunday School Association to work out a plan for the Colorado high schools. While these committees were at work, they learned of the North Dakota Bible study for credit plan. They discovered that the two plans had much in common. The Colorado plan provided a four-year elective study. The teaching was to be done in the churches during Sunday-school hours. The instruction was to comprise each year forty recitations of forty-five minutes. If the work was taken for credit, the teacher of the class must have: "The minimum scholastic attainment of high school teachers equivalent to graduation from a college belonging to the North Central Association of Colleges and Secondary Schools, including special training in the subjects they teach." This would tend to raise the standards of teaching in the Sunday schools where such courses were offered.

In 1915 there were eight hundred and fifty-six high school pupils enrolled throughout the state, of whom two hundred were Roman Catholics. The Kansas State Teachers' Association in 1914 passed a resolution favoring a similar program for their own state. However, the Colorado plan failed to develop into a movement. The reason was perhaps the new star that was rising on the eastern horizon, the weekday religious schools of Gary, Indiana.

V. *Origin of Weekday Church Schools.*

1. *The Gary plan.* Ideas, like some garden seeds, often take a long time to germinate. It was in 1905 that Dr. George U. Wenner of New York read a paper at the Inter-Church Conference in Carnegie Hall. The result was the passing of a resolution:

> Resolved, that in the need of more systematic education in religion, we recommend for favorable consideration of the public school authorities of this county the proposal to allow the children to absent themselves, without detriment, from the public school on Wednesday or some afternoon of the school week for the purpose of attending religious instruction in their own churches, and we urge upon the churches the advisability of availing themselves of the opportunity so granted to give instruction in addition to that given on Sunday.[5]

But adopting a resolution is one thing, and putting the contents of the resolution into operation is quite another matter. It was not before nine years later that a plan similar to the one proposed by Wenner was realized.

A Methodist pastor, J. M. Avann, and the superintendent of schools at Gary, Indiana, William Wirth, in the fall of 1913 discussed the possibility of a co-operation between the Gary churches and the public schools in adding religion to the courses of study for the children of their city. The result was that half a dozen churches of different denominations co-operated, and in the fall of 1914 the plan was put into operation. The following year four directors were engaged. The young industrial city of Gary soon found itself a center of interest, not merely because of its rapid growth, but because of its plan of weekday religious schools. Visitors from colleges and theological seminaries from all parts of the country came to study the Gary system of religion education.

---

[5] Foster Gift, *Weekday Religious Education*, p. 29.

2. *A nation-wide movement.* Gary did not have a patent on its plan, so other communities set up similar schools, some almost exact duplications, while others were modifications. The plans were tailored to fit local conditions. Some cities that early adopted the Gary plan are: Van Wert, Ohio; Toledo, Ohio; Rochester, New York; Minneapolis, Minnesota; Batavia, Illinois; Princeton, Illinois; Oak Park, Illinois. Twenty-five years ago classes were also begun as an experiment in the Lakeview area of Chicago, Illinois. William Bogan, superintendent of the Chicago schools, himself a Roman Catholic, gave his permission to this Protestant experiment of releasing children from the public schools one hour each week to receive religious instruction in local churches. The program is now sponsored by the church federation of the city and is shared by Roman Catholics and Protestants alike. New York City is another example of a large city that is sponsoring a program of religious educational co-operation between church and state.

At present the movement begun in Gary, Indiana, has become nation-wide; in all but two states we now find weekday religious schools. Although planned originally for the elementary-school level, the movement has expanded to the high-school level in some communities. These schools are conducted in rural as well as urban areas. Although the patterns vary, there are certain general principles that govern this church and state co-operation. The church provides the curriculum and teachers at no expense to the state. The state through its schools releases the pupils at the *written request of the parents.*

VI. *The McCollum Case.*

From time to time the legal and constitutional aspects of this church and state educational co-operation have been questioned. The matter came to a head in what has come to be called the *McCollum Case* in Champaign, Illinois. There have been law suits pertaining to the weekday schools throughout the land from New York to California, but the McCollum Case became the focus of the controversy because it was appealed to the United States Supreme Court.

Champaign, Illinois, sponsored a weekday program. The classes met in the *school buildings* on released time. James Terry McCollum, son of Vashti McCollum, entered the fourth grade of the district school in the fall of 1943. That semester he and five other children did not attend these religious classes. Having been transferred to another school the second semester, he found himself the only child in his class not enrolled for Christian education. James' mother brought suit against the Board of Education to prohibit the continuation of released time from the public school for religious purposes.

The Supreme Court of Illinois upheld the Board of Education. However, the case was then referred to the United States Supreme Court, where the decision of the Illinois Court was reversed. This came as a stunning blow to the teachers and directors of the weekday schools. A careful study of the opinion of the Supreme Court as pronounced by Justice Black seemed to indicate that it was not directed against the weekday church schools in general, but against the type of school conducted in Champaign. It was the use of public school buildings for religious instruction to which they objected:

> Here not only are the state's tax-supported buildings used for the dissemination of religious doctrines. The state also affords sectarian groups an invaluable aid in that it helps to provide pupils for the religious classes through use of the state's compulsory school machinery. This is not separation of Church and State.

When the leaders in the movement had recovered from the shock, they came to realize that it was not the principle of released time that was being judged, but the use of public school buildings for religious instruction.

VII. *Organization and Administration.*

Before the McCollum Case became a legal matter, a number of classes had been conducted in public school buildings. Now, however, they meet in churches. The advantages of having the classes meet in the regular school classrooms were:

1. It saved time in going to a neighboring church.
2. It tended to integrate the instruction with the other courses taught.
3. It helped to maintain an educationally accepted level of instruction.

The types of organization and administration vary. In some cities there is an Inter-faith (Christians, Roman Catholics, and Jews) Board, as in New York City, that directs the instruction. In other cities, as in Chicago, the schools are sponsored by the Church Federation. Some communities, including Indianapolis, have interdenominational boards that are altogether independent of local church federations. A few are independent ventures.

VIII. *Financial Support.*

The schools are financed in various ways. Co-operating churches in some instances include the weekday schools in their annual budget. Others make annual pledges to the work, although these are not included in the annual budget of the church. Special offerings are taken, especially at Thanksgiving Day union meetings. In some areas subscription drives are used as the main means of financial support. The most successful method seems to be for the co-operating churches to include the weekday schools in their annual budget. The schools are then spared a hand to mouth existence.

IX. *Curriculum.*

Attempts at preparing graded curricula acceptable to all concerned have not been altogether successful. In some communities the demand is for a strictly biblical curriculum; in others the request is for more general Christian instruction with pupil workbooks. The materials prepared by the International Council and published as co-operative texts have met with considerable favorable acceptance but also with some criticism.

X. *Teachers.*

One of the greatest problems of the weekday church schools is that of securing qualified teachers. The ideal is to engage as teachers those who have training equivalent to that of the public school teacher, with the addition of specialized training in Christian education. In many instances it is not possible to arrange a staggered schedule throughout the week, but the classes are conducted at the same hour and on the same day of the week in all the schools of the local system.[6] Hence a large staff of teachers is required. Students from Christian colleges and theological seminaries are recruited, but their own class schedules must be considered. Pastors and pastors' wives frequently serve, as do other members of the church staff. Volunteer teachers often do not measure up to educational standards.

XI. *The Tomorrow of Weekday Church Schools.*

The future of the weekday church schools is uncertain. There are some educational leaders who feel that they cannot survive, at least not in their present form. Although sponsored by the church, these schools are at the mercy of the state. To grant the schools a legal status is one thing, but to create a congenial co-operation between secular education and religious education is quite another matter. Without unnecessary worry about their tomorrow, these schools should strive to render a worthy service today. The areas which are in greatest need of improvement are the recruiting and

---

[6] In Chicago it is Wednesday afternoons from 2:00 to 3:15 p.m.

training of teachers, and the preparation of improved graded curricula.

REVIEW QUESTIONS

1. What is the weekday church school?
2. What is meant by the struggle between church and state?
3. What was Christ's attitude as to human responsibility to church and state?
4. What is the European plan?
5. How does our country deal with the problem?
6. To what denomination must our president belong?
7. What was the Spartan idea as to the child?
8. What was the Oregon case?
9. What bearing does it have on weekday schools?
10. What was the North Dakota plan?
11. What was the Colorado plan?
12. What was the Gary plan?
13. Who suggested something similar in 1905?
14. When did the Gary plan begin to operate?
15. How widespread is the movement today?
16. What was the McCollum case?
17. Why did the Supreme Court opinion not close all weekday church schools?
18. What were three advantages of conducting the classes in the public school buildings?
19. How are weekday church schools sponsored and administered?
20. How are funds secured?
21. What in general constitutes the curriculum?
22. How are teachers secured?
23. What are some of the problems of the recruitment of teachers?
24. What about the future of these schools?
25. What two areas of the schools need improvement?

QUESTIONS FOR DISCUSSION

1. What would be the advantages and disadvantages of conducting the weekday classes *after school hours?*
2. Some have suggested that Saturday forenoon be devoted to weekday religious instruction. Give your opinion of such a plan.
3. Some have proposed that a general course in religion be included in the regular curriculum of the public school, this to be taught without a denominational or sectarian bias. Give your opinion of such a proposal.

4. Give instances of courses now taught in the public schools that do have religious implications.
5. How would you proceed to launch a weekday program in your community?
6. Give examples of the co-operation of the church and state in our country.
7. How may the difficulties of an interdenominational curriculum be overcome?
8. Would weekly half-hour *religious assemblies* in the public schools serve the same purpose as classes?
9. What are the problems connected with having pastors teach weekday classes?
10. How would you answer the objection: "Until the church makes better use of its Sunday school, it has no right to ask the public school to release pupils to attend weekday religious classes"?

13

Christian Youth Camps

STUDY OUTLINE

I. *Origin.*

Man's original home was in a garden, not in a crowded city (Gen. 2:8). It was Cain who first "builded a city" (Gen. 4:17). Thus cities came into being early in the history of the human race. Families banded themselves together into villages for mutual protection from enemies. The development of industry and commerce has contributed to the growth of cities. The rapid population transfers from the rural to the urban areas in recent times have given sociologists and psychologists much concern. The city dweller is forced into an artificial type of life. The man who works in an air-conditioned office on the twentieth floor of a skyscraper and who ascends and descends by means of a mechanical elevator is a prisoner, whether he recognizes it or not. If in addition his family lives in a few small rooms in an apartment building, shared by a score or more families, the artificiality of his life becomes even more acute. The cities try to ease the conditions by providing parks and recreation centers, but these are crowded and tend to intensify the feeling of urban congestion.

The growing interest in summer youth-camps and family camping indicates the human need for a period of freedom, even if brief, from the confinement of urban life. The growing trend for city workers to live in the suburbs is not a mere real-estate business project. It is based on that human urge to return to rural freedom. Living in the suburbs provides the services of city conveniences, while enjoying a near approach to the country. This leaves the heart-of-the-city gospel ministry to slum missions and the Salvation Army, as the local churches are moved to where the congregations reside. The problem of ministering to the children of the city slums is a result of this trend.

Camping as a phase of religious education can be traced back to the Jewish Feast of Tabernacles. This was an annual family-camping experience dramatizing an important era of Hebrew history, the wilderness wanderings. For a whole week, seven days in the late summer, the Hebrew family moved out of doors and lived in tabernacles, booths constructed from the branches and twigs of trees (Lev. 23:33–44; John 7:2, 37). These booths were erected in the streets, outside the walls of Jerusalem, and on the flat roofs of the houses. Each day the congregation marched in a religious parade. The last day was considered the *great* day of the feast when there were special ceremonies. Since the festival came at harvest time, it was also a feast of thanksgiving for material blessings.

The origin of our *Christian* camping program is somewhat obscure. Some believe that it was the Methodist camp meetings common during the latter part of the nineteenth century. The entire family, together with food provisions and a tent, were loaded into the wagon drawn by horses, sometimes by oxen, and the family as a whole, children and grandparents, were transported sometimes a distance of many miles to the campground. This often consisted of an open space in the woods where the tents could be pitched. There was the central tabernacle, the place where the services were held, and at some camps there was also a *boarding tent* where unmarried people and others who had not brought provisions might share in a community table. Though the event was social as well as spiritual, the services were usually of the revival type. Sinners were converted, and backsliders were reclaimed. These camp meetings contributed much to the spiritual life of the local church.

At Des Plaines, Illinois, just outside of the city of Chicago, the Methodists established a campground in 1906. In the lease of the grounds there was a clause stipulating that "no games or other recreational features shall be permitted." There was evidently some fear that the camp might become recreational rather than spiritual. Youth, however, finds a way to get what it wants, so an adjoining cornfield was secured as a *play field*. In the place of tents, a frame tabernacle and cottages were built. Today the camp services are continued each summer, but with a change in objective and emphasis. The mourners' bench and the altar call are now matters of history, rather than of present practice.

The Salvation Army has for many years conducted its *Fresh-Air Camps* for mothers and children from the slum areas of our large cities. This has been both a social and a spiritual service.

The Boy and Girl Scouts, especially the former, have developed a camping program which, though not directly religious in objective, is nevertheless constructive and morally wholesome.

The Chautauqua movement, though not basically a project in camping, was an out-of-doors program of religious education. It was founded in 1874, at Lake Chautauqua in New York, near the city of Jamestown, by Bishop Vincent and Lewis Miller. This developed into what became known as the Chautauqua Movement and spread throughout the country. As it expanded, the movement took on a cultural rather than a spiritual tone. Lecturers, singers, musicians, and others made up the Chautauqua staff. The movement lost its popular appeal with the advent of the movies, radio, and so forth, but the Chautauqua summer sessions are annually conducted on the Chautauqua grounds at the lake from which it received its name.

It is the YMCA that has contributed most to the promotion of the camping movement. In fact, it has established a pattern that most camps have adopted with some minor modifications. The YMCA owns and operates a number of summer camps popularly known as "Y Camps." College Camp, or George Williams Camp, as it is also called, located on Lake Geneva, Wisconsin, is perhaps one of the best known, partly because of its central location. Then there is the camp in Estes Park, Colorado, in the heart of the Rocky Mountains, and another on the beautiful shores of Lake Winnepesaukee in New Hampshire, to mention only three of the many.

Christian youth camps, sponsored by denominations, had their origin shortly after the First World War. Most of the denominations now conduct such camps. Often it is the conference that owns and operates the camps. One denomination with eleven conferences has a conference-owned campground in every conference (The Evangelical Covenant Church of America). One of these conferences owns two camps, while another, a large one, owns several.

In addition to these denominational camps, there are interdenominational camps owned and operated by private corporations. The Winona Lake Bible Conference grounds in Indiana; the Maranatha Bible Conference Camp near Muskegon, Michigan; the Canadian Keswick Bible Camp on the Muskoka Lakes in Ontario, Canada, are examples of this type.

Summer conferences conducted on the campuses of Christian schools, as, for instance, the Northfield Conference held annually on the grounds of the Northfield school at Northfield, Massachusetts, can scarcely be called camps, even though some of the conferees live in tents. The buildings of the school are used for housing and feeding as well as for the services.

II. *Types.*

1. *Young people's camps.* In our study we shall confine ourselves to the denominational camps which follow a general pattern. For a number of years the camps recruited young people eighteen years of age and up. Very often the "ups" outnumbered those who were in the younger age bracket. The programs were geared to the interests, needs, and understanding of young people. More recently other types of camps have emerged.

2. *High school age.* There is the high school age camp. For a time an attempt was made to recruit this age group for the young people's camp. This necessitated in some instances a dual program, since the high school freshman was bored by the type of lectures and studies that challenged the college senior. Experience proved that it was better, whenever possible, to conduct two separate camps, one for the high-school age, the other for young people.

3. *Children's camps.* The success of these high school age camps led to introducing children's camps where children in the upper grades of the elementary school might attend. The popularity of these children's camps with both parents and children has been phenomenal.

4. *Family camps.* A fourth type of summer camp is the family camp. Young parents who have enjoyed the young people's camps before they were married are often attracted to the family camps. They may have first met at a camp and are still interested in camp activities, so they bring their families. Provision is made for play supervision of the children while the parents attend the sessions.

5. *Winter camps.* There is a fifth type that is rapidly becoming popular, the winter camp. These are usually week-end events beginning on Friday evening, continuing through Saturday, and con-

cluding with the Sunday forenoon service attended at a neighboring church or at the camp chapel. Skating, skiing, tobogganing, and other winter sports constitute the Saturday daylight-period program, with Bible study, discussion, and devotions during the long evening hours of Friday and Saturday. The winter camp calls for cottages and chapels that can be kept comfortable and warm even in severe weather. But since the attendance is usually not large, only a small part of the camp needs to be winterized. There should always be a nurse available to give first aid to broken limbs, sprained ankles, and similar casualties. January and February are the popular months for these winter camps. In some parts of the country November and December may be included.

III. *Objectives.*

If Christian youth camps are to make a contribution to the total program of Christian education, the leaders must be conscious of definite goals. What is the church attempting to achieve through these camps? What changes do we anticipate in the conduct and character of those who share in the camping experience? If we have definite objectives before us as we plan our camping program we shall, at the close of the camp, better be able to evaluate the effectiveness of this phase of Christian education. Charles W. Eliot of Harvard once referred to camping as "America's greatest contribution to education." But just how and what does the Christian youth camp contribute to the ongoing work of the Christian church?

Raymond Peters, in his compact volume, *Let's Go Camping*, suggests the following ten goals for Christian camps.[1]

1. To discover the laws of God operating through nature and to utilize as fully as possible the opportunities for developing religious experience through contacts with nature.
2. To provide group experience in Christian living; to learn how to live together happily and well.
3. To provide increased knowledge of the Bible and its meaning for life.
4. To broaden Christian fellowship through interracial, interfaith, interclass, and international relationships.
5. To provide experiences in co-operative group work projects and labor for the good of the camp group and the larger community.
6. To enrich and increase the knowledge which a Christian

---

[1] pp. 20–21.

ought to possess in regard to faith and practice, particularly those aspects of knowledge and understanding which are not likely to be acquired elsewhere.

7. To lead individuals to make a personal commitment to Christ.
8. To help the camper develop a program of personal growth and Christian action.
9. To direct each individual in camp experience so that he may make a more effective contribution to his home, church, and community.
10. To discover persons possessing potential leadership qualities; to give them leadership training and enlist them in definite forms of Christian service.

These ten objectives are comprehensive and far reaching. No camp would perhaps attempt to attain all ten in one camping season, but there are some which should be aimed at in every camp. Reduced to simple categories these might be: 1) wholesome recreation; 2) Christian fellowship; 3) Christian nurture; 4) evangelism.

IV. *Program.*

If these goals are to be attained, there is need for a directed but not regimented program. Rules and regulations are necessary in order to facilitate harmonious group-living while in camp. But regulations must be more than an array of inhibitions. The counselee who reads or hears his counselor recite a long list of things that the camper must *not* do may not express in words his mental response to this fence of inhibitions, but there are inner, unspoken protests. A Christian summer camp must not even remotely suggest a concentration camp, but on the other hand it should not suggest unlimited freedom.

Rules and regulations should be for the safety and general good of all campers. In some camps the specific rules are drawn up by a committee consisting of the counselors and a few counselees selected, not by the administration, but by the groups they represent. This is a democratic method which has been found effective. When counselees have helped to formulate the rules governing the camp, they are more inclined to obey them.

V. *Ownership versus Renting of Camp.*

Economy-minded church leaders have raised the question whether or not the church is justified in investing so much money in a camp which is in operation only two months of the year and for ten months stands idle. The answer would be that it depends upon the significance of the work that is accomplished during the two months. A farmer invests a large sum of money in a piece of machinery, it may be a combine, which he uses for only a few days each season, but it saves so much labor that, in spite of the cost, it is considered a wise investment. A serious evaluation will no doubt bring us to the conclusion that the summer camp is a good investment for the church because of what it does for its youth. Christ evaluated one soul as being worth more than heaven and earth. What, then, if that soul is a young person who has a life to invest in the cause of Christ and his church?

There is another related question. Is the church justified in investing in the purchase and operation of its own camp if it can make use of the camp grounds and facilities owned by others? There are arguments both for and against such a venture.

1. *Arguments against.*

a. The camp represents a large investment of money in property that lies idle ten months of the year. This money could be used for missions or home-land evangelism or perhaps the addition of better facilities for the teaching ministry in the local churches.

b. It is not merely the original cost that must be considered, but the upkeep as well. The deterioration of buildings is rapid. Equipment must be replaced from time to time. A custodian of the property must be secured for the entire year.

c. If you conduct your camp on rented grounds, you need not meet every year at the same place, but may occasionally vary the location. This may stimulate a new interest.

d. If you own a camp and lease it to other groups, it is difficult to control the conduct of the conferees. Some youth groups have very liberal standards as to recreation, conduct, and Christianity in general.

e. If someone else owns the campgrounds, you are spared a lot of worry and expense. In some camps the only concern of the leaders of the visiting group is to register the individual campers, prepare a program, and secure the staff of teachers and counselors. The housing and feeding is cared for in every detail by the managers of the camp.

2. *Arguments for.*

a. If you own your own grounds you may arrange your camping schedule to suit your convenience.

b. You may receive revenue by renting it to other groups and so fill in a full two-month schedule.

c. You may set your own rules and regulations for controlling the camp. Rising and retiring hours may be adjusted according to the age of the counselees.

d. You may reduce the cost to each camper by operating on a cost and no-profit plan.

e. You may plan the buildings, grounds, and equipment to suit the needs of your constituency.

3. *How to secure a camp.*

The problem of how a church group may secure its own camp-grounds is not easily solved. Even within a group of Christian leaders there will arise tensions because of differences of opinion. There is the matter of having the camp centrally located, the matter of transportation, original cost, and so forth. A campground may be secured in various ways.

a. Nonpaying or poorly paying summer resorts may at times be purchased for a small expenditure of cash and on easy terms.

b. Old estates located on lake property are sometimes for sale. The buildings may be remodeled.

c. Fully equipped camps may be purchased from some other church group or private corporation.

d. A camp site may be donated to the group with the understanding that buildings are to be erected by those who receive the gift.

e. A desirable camp site may be purchased and the buildings and equipment added to suit the needs and the funds available.

4. *Suggestions for selecting a camp.*

In the purchase of campgrounds, there are some things that need to be investigated.

a. *Drainage.* Is the soil clay or gravel? Do not buy during the winter months or after prolonged dry weather. A site that seems highly desirable after two weeks of dry weather may become a swamp towards the close of a week of continuous rain.

b. *Water.* Is the water safe for drinking and cooking? Is there always an adequate supply even in dry weather? Is it derived from a well, spring, or lake? Is the well deep or shallow? Is there water for swimming or bathing? Is there a real lake, or is it a swimming hole that easily becomes polluted, or in dry seasons becomes a stagnant pool or goes altogether dry?

c. *Plumbing.* If the buildings are old, the plumbing should be carefully examined. Replacing the plumbing in a camp may prove to be very expensive.

d. *Hazards.* Are there railroads or heavily traveled highways adjacent to the camp that would endanger the lives of children campers? Is the swimming safe as to the depth of the water and the swiftness of the current? Are there poison oak, poison ivy, or similar obnoxious plants on or near the grounds?

e. *Proximity to cities and towns.* If the camp is near to a city or town there will be the problem of keeping the counselees on the grounds. They will be tempted to go to these trading centers for refreshments and recreation, thus failing to share in the full program of the camp.

f. *General location.* Are the grounds centrally located in the area from which you will receive your counselees? A good camp-ground, but poorly located, may prove to become unpopular with youth.

g. *Transportation.* Are there convenient all-weather roads, or do they become almost impassable for cars after prolonged wet weather? Are there bus and train connections not too far from camp? Are the schedules of these buses and trains convenient for counselees? Trains and buses that arrive in the middle of the night or the wee hours of the morning may create a real problem in the coming and going of especially the younger group.

h. *Environment.* Are there taverns, public dance halls, and similar places of evil influence in the vicinity of the camp? On the lakes this is often a problem. The music from a tavern or dance hall across the lake will scarcely add to the spirit of worship in a service conducted in camp.

i. *Age and condition of buildings.* Check carefully on roofs and floors. A roofing job the first or second year of the ownership of the camp may come as an embarrassing unexpected expense. Since most camp buildings are made of lumber, it is well to check for termites.

j. *Terms of the purchase contract.* Study carefully the contract before signing it. The seller may have no intention of deceiving you, but do not fail to read every word of the document you signed, even the small print. The payments may seem small and extend over a long period of time, but the interest you promise to pay may add up to a considerable sum. It is wise to consult a lawyer before concluding the deal. There are such problems as securing a clear title to the property. The property may be mortgaged and the terms of the mortgage be quite different from the contract you have with the one who sells.

On the committee appointed to secure a camp there should, if possible, be a carpenter or even better, a builder, competent to evaluate the property. If you rent a camp site, insist upon a written contract. Oral agreements, though given in good faith, are subject to misunderstanding.

VI. *The Camp Staff.*

1. *Kitchen crew.* If possible, the same cook and assistants should be engaged for the entire season. Permitting each camp to provide its own kitchen staff has not proved successful. Good food, well prepared, makes or breaks the reputation of a camp. One week of poor food in camp may harm the reputation of the camp for years to come. Balanced meals are a must.

2. *Camp director (dean).* This is not the manager of the grounds and equipment but a person who is responsible for the comfort of the counselees and the carrying out of the program for the week. The camp director is often a clergyman with a keen interest in youth.

3. *Camp nurse.* If the camp is large, a doctor too may be needed. No matter how small the camp, there should always be a nurse on the grounds. She should not be loaded with other responsibilities, but given both time and a place for her work. Many campgrounds are provided with a resident nurse for the season. In children's camps it is a growing policy for each child to bring a health certificate from the family physician.

4. *Recreational director.* Although the recreational program is usually planned by a committee, it should be directed by one person. Physical education teachers in the public schools are often available for such camps. The program must be of such a nature that all counselees can participate with some degree of enjoyment. The type of game or athletics where a few stars demonstrate should be avoided. Counselors have been known to become so engrossed in some game of tennis or croquet played with some fellow counselor, that the counselees have been neglected and have become but watchers of the game. A certain amount of competition is good, games between counselees and counselors are at times interesting, but one must studiously avoid creating a feeling of frustration on the part of those who are not skilled.

5. *Musical director.* Young people like to sing, but unless direction is given to the musical program of a youth camp, it may quickly deteriorate into cheap gospel-jazz. The musical director should inspire the youth, not merely to sing, but to choose truly Christian music. Gospel choruses may be used effectively in camp if they are carefully selected. Sometimes well-meaning musical directors in youth camps develop an antagonistic attitude towards the best in church music by not recognizing the place of some of the more popular gospel hymns. Musical taste cannot be legislated, it must be cultivated.

6. *Chaplain.* The Chaplain may be one of the pastors of the

co-operating churches. He need not, and should not, lead every worship service himself, but rather assume the responsibility to secure someone to do so. Pastors and counselees may be recruited for such worship leadership. The chaplain may serve as counselor at large, with definite "office" hours in his cabin when individuals may come to him with their problems.

7. *Teachers.* The teaching staff may be made up of local pastors and youth leaders, with the addition of one or two *outside speakers.* A new face and a new voice adds interest to a camp. It is wise not to load any teacher too heavily with speaking or teaching assignments. Even though well prepared before he comes to camp, the outside speaker will find it necessary to modify and adjust his messages to fit the local situation. A Bible teacher and a missionary speaker, together with local pastors, may constitute the teaching staff. The Bible teacher may be a local pastor, while the visitor may be the speaker at the vesper services. A recently returned young missionary may contribute much to a youth camp. The messages should be brief and well illumined with illustrations and instructive stories.

8. *Counselors.* The failure or success of a youth camp is largely dependent upon the choice of counselors. These should be carefully selected long enough in advance of the camp season so that they may familiarize themselves with their duties. The panicky drafting of counselors on the eve of the camp, and even after the camp has begun, does not promote worth-while camping experiences. The counselor is not to serve as a policeman to discover violators of camp rules and regulations. His function is to serve as a guide so that the counselees will get as much as possible out of their camping. He lives with his group and shares its experiences. In camps using the cabin unit, there will be one counselor for each cabin.

VII. *The Overhead Organization.*

The camp is owned by some corporate church organization. This organization will have a board or committee, elected or appointed, that is responsible for the physical phase of the grounds. A camp business manager is chosen and given the responsibility for the purchasing of supplies and the hiring of help. This should not be a year by year arrangement with a new manager each year. He should serve on a full-time basis. In some instances, the manager lives on the grounds during the entire year and serves as general custodian.

The camp program is usually planned by some committee. The

leaders, counselors, teachers, and preachers are selected and engaged. They assume responsibility for publicity and preregistration. When the camp opens, the counselees have already been assigned to their respective counselors and cabins. The work of registration at the opening of the camp is thus greatly facilitated.

Accounts are carefully kept and books audited. A financial report should be published annually. Those who support the project have a right to know the financial status of their investment. Christian stewardship includes an accurate accounting of how the Lord's money has been spent as well as contributing financially to the work of the church.

REVIEW QUESTIONS

1. What annual camping season was observed by the Hebrews?
2. What was the nature of the Methodist camp meetings?
3. When was the Des Plaines Methodist Camp established?
4. What provision did it offer for recreation?
5. What has the Salvation Army contributed to camping?
6. When was the Chautauqua movement founded?
7. Where?
8. Who were the two leaders?
9. What religious group has contributed most to the camping movement?
10. Name three of its camps.
11. Name three interdenominational camps.
12. Name five types of camps.
13. What did President Eliot of Harvard say about camps?
14. What ten objectives does Raymond Peters give for camps?
15. Into what four categories may they be grouped?
16. Why are camp rules necessary?
17. What may counselees contribute to the formulation of such rules?
18. Give five arguments against a conference owning its own camp.
19. Give five arguments for it.
20. State five ways of securing a camp.
21. State ten things to observe in choosing a camp.
22. Name the necessary staff members.
23. How should a camp be governed?
24. How should counselors be distributed in camp?
25. What does the Christian stewardship of money include?

Questions For Discussion

1. Prepare a set of helpful rules for directing the conduct of campers.
2. Outline a schedule of activities for a day in camp.
3. What are the advantages of having a number of small cabins rather than a large dormitory?
4. Should children's camps provide for a visitors' day in the middle of the camp week when parents may visit?
5. How should the Sunday schedule of activities differ from the daily schedule?
6. What would you consider the ideal number of campers in order to secure the best results?
7. What is the difference between a *conference* and a *camp?*
8. How would you select your camp counselors?
9. Should the tuition paid by campers be only enough to pay for the current expense of the camp, or should it also contribute towards the original cost and upkeep of the grounds?
10. Using an outline map of the United States, locate the camps owned and operated by the conferences of your denomination. Indicate the area each camp serves.

14

The Christian Press

STUDY OUTLINE

I. **Importance**
 1. The p o w e r of the printed page
 2. The daily newspapers
 3. Magazines and periodicals
 4. Publishing houses (volume of production)
 5. The gospel in print

II. **Types**
 1. Curriculum materials
 2. Fiction
 3. Pamphlets
 4. Newspapers and periodicals
 5. Devotional literature
 6. The gospel tract

III. **Distribution of Christian Literature**
 1. Mail order
 2. Over-the-counter bookstores
 3. Local-church book tables
 4. Colporteurs

I. *Importance.*

In evaluating the agencies that contribute to Christian education, the influence of the Christian press is often overlooked. In spite of radio and audio-visual programs, the press still wields a subtle, though silent, influence. The tons of Christian literature that are annually ground out from the printing presses find readers as well as purchasers. The Bible itself, the best seller, is a product of the religious press. A perusal of the seasonal catalogs distributed by the publishing houses and religious bookstores will convey some idea of the volume as well as variety of Christian publications. There are more than fifty denominational publishing agencies besides those of nondenominational and interdenominational scope. They publish materials in the fields of theology, history, biography, fiction, poetry, devotions, and so forth. Then there are the daily, weekly, monthly, quarterly, and annual publications, besides pamphlets and tracts of almost every description.

1. *The power of the press.*

The power of the press to mold public opinion is at times actually alarming. The daily newspapers read by millions of gullible Americans deal with political, social, economic, and religious issues. Many of these readers rarely take time for the editorials, but they devour

179

the dramatized and often glamorized news items, both domestic and foreign, and chuckle at the cartoons and the comic strips. They never stop to think that the news items have taken on psychological color as they are reported, and that cartoons are subtly loaded with political propaganda.

2. *Daily papers.* There are approximately 18,000 daily newspapers in the United States. Every day they contribute to the education of the people, developing attitudes and modifying public opinion. Even in the enlightened twentieth century there are many who believe that whatever appears in printer's ink must be true.

3. *Magazines and periodicals.* Besides the dailies, the American reading public consumes the contents of a variety of magazines. In 1958 the circulation statistics were as follows:

Life — 5,851,168
Ladies' Home Journal — 5,448,570
Saturday Evening Post — 5,152,891
Look — 5,006,348
Farm Journal — 3,533,956
Coronet — 2,891,337

The Marvel Comic Group tops them all with 6,499,375. Since each copy of a magazine is read, at least in part, by several members of the same family, the influence is multiplied far beyond that of the number of copies printed and sold. Add to this the large volumes of so-called pulp magazines that are sold on the public news stands and read by children and youth.

4. *Publishing houses.* In addition to the newspapers and periodicals, some good and some bad, there are, in our country, about one hundred and fifty book publishers. The number of titles published each year is almost unbelievable. The following approximate figures for 1957 have been taken from the *Publishers' Weekly,* January 20, 1958:

The Macmillan Company	401 titles
Harper and Brothers	349 "
McGraw-Hill	311 "
Doubleday & Company	299 "
Oxford University Press	257 "

These five publishing houses together publish annually more than 1,600 titles, not to mention those by smaller publishers. The publishing of religious books is in no wise limited to the denominational or religious publishers, for many of the large publishers have departments of religious literature also.

There is, however, an increasing number of "dime novels" still published. They have advanced in price and have deteriorated in content. They are eagerly devoured by children and youth who have not learned to discriminate in their choice of reading matter. The recommended lists of books for collateral reading used in our public high schools contain the titles of books that a few years ago would have been considered unfit for adolescent consumption. There is no excuse for modern educators permitting, much less requiring, our adolescents to drag their minds through such literary muck for the sake of sampling realism.

People will read whatever materials are at hand when the urge to read is felt. Children and youth will read good books if they are interesting and conveniently at hand. The biblical saying, "For as he thinketh within himself, so is he" (Prov. 23:7), might well have added to it, "A man thinketh within himself that which he readeth."

5. *The gospel in print.* With an American public that the public schools have taught how to read, and the spread of questionable, not to say pornographic literature, both legally and illegally available, the Christian press has a real mission to perform.

In the gospel ministry of the Christian church the printed page has some advantages over the oral message. In the first place, there is the permanency of the message. The message may be read and reread years, even centuries, after the messenger has died. We now have available for study in addition to the Bible itself, sermons by Calvin, Luther, the Wesleys, Jonathan Edwards, Dwight L. Moody, just to mention a few. An oral message tends to diminish in power after the sound waves have been spent. The printed message may grow and become revitalized as it is read and reread.

In the second place, the printed page safeguards the contents. An oral message is often misquoted, words are accidentally omitted or added. The printed page may be misinterpreted, but not misquoted. When a word, phrase, or sentence has been set in type and recorded in printer's ink it is like the laws of the Medes and the Persians.

In the third place, the printed page encourages a private perusal. A tract may be accepted, pocketed, and then later be read in private. Likewise the spiritual message of a good book may become vitalized as it is read in solitude.

There is a fourth advantage in the printed page—its ease of circulation through the mails. A gospel tract may be enclosed with a personal letter and mailed at no extra cost. A book may be ordered from a New York bookstore and delivered by the rural free delivery to a farm home in western Kansas. Good books make good Christmas or birthday gifts and can conveniently be sent through the mails.

II. *Types.*

1. *Curriculum materials.* The publishing of textbooks for Christian colleges, theological seminaries, and Bible institutes is an expanding project. Then there are tracts and pamphlets, besides local-church weekly bulletins and monthly or quarterly papers. The bulk of publishing is, however, in the field of books intended for Christians in general. Sunday school, vacation Bible school lessons, and youth programs constitute much of the published materials.

2. *Fiction.* Christian fiction is an ever expanding field. Perhaps the best known of the Christian fiction of a generation ago is *In His Steps* by Charles M. Sheldon. This book had its origin in Topeka, Kansas, where Sheldon, as the pastor of a local church, gave a series of talks to his young people on the general theme, "What Would Jesus Do?" Contests in the writing of fiction with a definite spiritual impact has uncovered a number of able and interesting writers in that field.

3. *Pamphlets.* The Protestant Reformation was promoted to a large extent through the pamphleteering of Luther, Erasmus, and Melanchthon. It is Luther's thesis nailed on the church door that is usually given as the beginning of the Reformation, but it was these religious pamphlets that carried the sparks of thought out to the public. John Foxe (1516–1587) broke forth in an eulogy of the press: "God hath opened the press to preach, whose voice the pope is never able to stop with all the puissance of his triple crown. By this printing, as by the gift of tongues and as by the singular organ of the Holy Spirit, the doctrine of the Gospel soundeth to all nations and countries under heaven."

In 1542 the English parliament passed an act giving the crown the absolute right to regulate printing. As a result there was a large number of anonymous pamphlets. Much of the printing in English was done in the early seventeenth century by the Pilgrim Press of Leyden, Holland, since that country had no restrictions on publishing. The earliest colonial literature was printed in the mother country, England. Alexander Whitaker, minister in Virginia, in 1613 published a tract that was printed in England. It was a plea for men and money to promote missionary work among the American Indians. In 1638 Stephen Day, an English printer, migrated to the new country and located in Boston. In 1639 he published what is claimed to be the first book printed in colonial America, the *Bay State Psalm Book,* a translation of the psalms in English meter. The book contained three hundred pages. Jesse Glover, a wealthy English dissenter, set out for America equipped with a font of type and money for a printing press. On the way to New England he died, but the equipment and a printer arrived safely. Glover's widow later married Henry Dunster who had the previous year become president of Harvard College. Thus the Harvard University Press had its humble origin.

The publishing of tracts and theological pamphlets kept the public informed on current theological trends and issues. Cotton Mather is credited with having written three hundred and eighty-two pamphlets, and Increase Mather with eighty-five. The first newspaper published in America, in Boston in 1690, *Public Occurrences*, was spiritual in tone and content. The purposes for its publication reflect this spirit: "That Memorable Occurrents of Divine Providence may not be neglected or Forgotten, as they too often are . . . . that something may be done toward curing or at least curbing the Charming of that Spirit of Lying which prevails among us."[1]

American independence was expressed religiously in the large number of Christian periodicals. Most of these projects died in their infancy. Private ventures failed for lack of financial support. One editor, desperate in his attempt to collect from his subscribers, addressed them thus:

> To Our Delinquent Subscribers: Beloved, I so call you because it is my vocation, and a habit. But there would be more sincerity in the phrase if you all had paid me. . . . As for the patronage of which you talk, whip me those patrons who do not pay. I would none of them. You owe me among you $3,000. I hope that your opulence is such, that it seems a trifling matter to you. The withholding your individual subscriptions may be a trifle and sport to you; but the deficit of the sum is death to me.[2]

4. *Newspapers and periodicals.* T. DeWitt Talmage, in 1871, declared in a public sermon that probably not more than five religious newspapers in the land were self-supporting. When the larger denominations began to publish their own periodicals, there was added a feeling of financial security. The Methodist *Advocate* within five years of its founding had a circulation of 25,000. The Protestant Episcopal Church, in 1804, launched the *Churchman's Magazine*, now the *Churchman*.

The Baptists, through the merger of a number of their publications, finally produced the *Watchman-Examiner*. Other denomina-

---

[1] Frederic Hudson, *Journalism in the United States from 1690 to 1872.*
[2] *Western Monthly Review*, edited by Thomas Fluit.

tions have passed through similar experiences where rival papers representing their own denomination, but functioning as private corporations, have either succumbed or yielded to mergers. At present practically all denominations have their own organs of printed communications owned and operated by the denomination and controlled by an editing committee or board.

In addition there are nondenominational publications, some liberal in their theological interpretations, some conservative, and some following a middle-of-the-road policy. Among such we find *Christian Century,* formerly the organ of the Disciples of Christ but now nondenominational, *Missionary Review of the Word, Christian Herald, Sunday School Times,* and *Christianity Today.*

Then there are cults and sects. We are familiar with the street-corner vendor who offers *The Watchtower* for sale, the mouthpiece of Jehovah's Witnesses. Mary Baker Eddy, in 1883, established the *Christian Science Journal;* in 1898 came the *Christian Science Sentinel,* a weekly. Finally, in 1908, two years before her death, Mrs. Eddy saw her dream of a daily newspaper realized in the *Christian Science Monitor,* which is considered as one of the best-edited daily newspapers in America.

At one time the denominational papers were not only self-supporting; they earned profits. At present most of the denominational publications receive annual subsidies from their respective denominations.

The modern religious periodical has taken on color both figuratively and literally. The format has been changed. The literary style has been improved. Colored ink and pictures have added to the cost of production, but also to the attractiveness of the printed product. Editors are men trained in modern journalism. The idea of having retired clergymen and former missionaries responsible for producing the denominational periodical is now largely a matter of past history. They are retained as contributing editors, but not as the ones responsible for the layout and general content.

Large publishing houses such as Abingdon Press, Augsburg Publishing House, Judson Press, Pilgrim Press, Revell, and Westminster Press, to name only a few of the many, operate according to established policies and principles. The smaller denominations have a democratic form of control. The editor in chief is elected by the denomination. A board or committee on publications meets at regular intervals of time to discuss policies, which are usually quite flexible, and determine what publications shall be undertaken. There are some that are essential to the work of the denomination and must be published whether they will pay for themselves or not; the denomination then grants a subsidy.

Retired clergymen sometimes get an idea that they should write autobiographies. The memories from their childhood and youth become vivid and seem to be so important that they feel these experiences should be shared with their contemporaries and preserved for the coming generation. But what seems to be significant to the autobiographer may have little if any interest to others, except to intimate friends and members of the immediate family. The publishing of such autobiographies would be poor financial ventures.

Then there are active clergymen who have some theological ax to grind. They are anxious to get their views into print. If it is a live controversial issue, the book might be a good financial risk, but what about the effect that it would have on the denomination? Would it create schisms and promote controversy? The same applies to controversial articles submitted to the editor for printing in the current denominational papers. How far should free utterance be permitted on controversial issues? When must a moratorium be declared on such debate? Should the editor shoulder the responsibility alone, or should he refer the matter to his board? Besides journalistic training, the religious editor needs to be well informed in theology. One prerequisite for holding the position of editor might well be a formal theological training.

There are other problems, for instance, that of advertising. Should a Christian paper accept well-paying advertisements of patent medicines? To what extent should the paper investigate the integrity of its advertisers? When the price of paper and the wages of linotypists and pressmen rise, should the subscription price also rise? Is there a ceiling beyond which the publishers dare not go? Must the size of the paper be reduced in order to meet this increase in cost?

5. *Devotional literature.* Within recent years there has been a growing demand for family worship helps in the form of inexpensive books or quarterlies containing daily meditations. The best known is perhaps the quarterly magazine, now bi-monthly, *The Upper Room,* begun by the Southern Methodists in 1935, and now published in Braille as well as in a number of different languages. Its circulation has passed the million mark. In general content it is interdenominational. Some denominations publish books of daily meditations with a daily prayer list for Christian leaders in their particular denomination.[3] This may limit the circulation,

---

[3] *The Covenant Home Altar,* Covenant Press, circulation 23,000 copies.

but it adds to its practical value in that it daily reminds those who use it of the institutions and leaders in the denomination. Even the children are thus made familiar with these names as they become the objects of family prayers.

6. *The tract.* One of the gospel agents of the Christian press is the tract. Throughout the history of Protestantism tracts have wielded a great influence. The tract has still a mission to perform. There are certain advantages in the use of the gospel tract in the program of evangelism. First of all they are convenient to handle, in the second place they are inexpensive, and in the third place they present a brief gospel message.

There are societies which specialize in the preparation, publishing, and distribution of tracts. One of the best known, perhaps, is the *Chicago Tract Society* which for several years has offered a prize for tracts of superior quality. One of the early winning tracts was one entitled "The Bread of Life" written by Charles Hjerpe, professor emeritus of North Park College (Chicago). This tract has been translated and is published in six languages. A recent prize winner, "Marred and Made Again," was written by a navy chaplain, Paul F. Erickson.

A number of inferior tracts have been printed and circulated. The literary style has been poor, the print job has been inferior, and the paper used has been cheap. The result has been that the gospel of Jesus Christ has been presented in an unattractive manner. It would have been far better to have published fewer tracts, but tracts that are attractive.

The following suggestions may be helpful in the choice of tracts:

1. *It should be attractive* (form). The quality of paper, type, and format are all important.
2. *It should be interesting* (content). A story or incident well told will tend to arrest and hold the attention.
3. *Its language should be dignified yet simple.* Avoid technical theological or psychological terms.
4. *It should be brief.* The four-page tract seems to be the most popular. A two-page tract usually fails to have enough content. An expanded tract becomes a pamphlet.
5. *It should present the gospel briefly but clearly.* Focusing the attention upon one carefully selected Bible passage is usually more effective than using several.

Gospel tracts should not be handed out promiscuously. Standing outside of a church or gospel tabernacle handing out gospel tracts to all who pass by may at first seem to be a worthy mission, but when one later discovers the way discarded tracts litter the sidewalks and the printed gospel is trodden under foot, it creates a disturbing impression. A few suggestions for the worthy use of good tracts may not be amiss:

1. Select your tracts carefully. Never give away a tract that you have not yourself studied carefully.

2. Classify the tracts. There are some tracts that are addressed especially to young people, some to the "down and outs," some to Christians. Some have as their objective to warn, others to encourage.

3. Use tracts sparingly but prayerfully.

4. Every evangelical church should have a tract box. This should be a neat, attractive dispenser of the gospel. Place it in such a position that interested persons may help themselves as they leave the church. Place the boxes high enough so that small children do not remove the tracts and scatter them on the floor.

5. Have a tract committee that keeps the box supplied. An almost empty tract-dispenser does not necessarily mean that there has been a great demand for tracts, but rather that the persons responsible have been careless.

6. Check through the box at least once a week for two reasons: first, to learn what type of tract is of greatest interest to those who attend your services; and second, to watch for *tares sown with the wheat.* Visitors of strange sects have been known to visit evangelical churches and smuggle their own brand of trade into the tract boxes.

III. *Distribution.*

Christian literature is usually distributed in four ways:

1. First of all there are the denominational bookstores who do a large mail-order business, besides the across-the-counter sales. During special seasons, such as Christmas and Easter, the volume of mail-order business is very large. Seasonal catalogs are published and mailed to local pastors and other church leaders.

2. Then there are the public religious bookstores, privately owned and operated. They have the advantage over the denominational sales centers in that the people of the community can come in and browse around and thus see what they buy.

3. There is a third agency, and that is the local church and conference bookshops. Some churches provide a book table where the worshipers may purchase their books. Some member of the church is in charge, and any profits go to the local church fund. At conventions and conferences a bookshop is set up, usually supplied

and operated by some representative of the denominational bookstore. Books written by a conference speaker or books dealing with some theme discussed during the sessions are usually featured. Such book tables and shops contribute much towards the distribution of Christian literature.

4. The colporteur is the house-to-house distributer of religious literature. Some of these carry samples and take orders to be delivered later. Others conduct a cash-and-carry business. Before the advent of the automobile, the horse-drawn "bookstores" circulated in rural communities. Although religious sects thus spread their propaganda, it is nevertheless true that these colporteurs rendered a real gospel service. Families that very rarely visited the larger cities or shopped at the religious bookstores became familiar with good Christian literature through these itinerant salesmen.

Review Questions

1. Approximately how many denominational publishing houses are there?
2. How many daily newspapers?
3. In the 1950 statistics, what three periodicals had the greatest circulation?
4. About how many book publishers are there in our country?
5. How many titles of books do the five largest publishing houses produce annually?
6. What is the value of a printed message over one delivered orally?
7. Who wrote *In His Steps?*
8. How did the book originate?
9. When did the English parliament give the control of printing to the crown?
10. What was the result?
11. Who was Stephen Day?
12. What was the origin of the Harvard University Press?
13. What did Talmage say in 1871 about the financial success of religious newspapers?
14. What is considered one of the best-edited daily newspapers in America?
15. What is the *Upper Room?*
16. What is perhaps the best-known publisher of tracts?
17. Give five criteria for choosing tracts.
18. What is a tract box?
19. Where should it be placed?
20. What is the function of a tract committee?

21. Name four agencies for distributing Christian literature.
22. When is the mail-order business at its peak?
23. What is the advantage of a local bookstore?
24. What is a colporteur?
25. Did he render his greatest service in urban or rural areas?

QUESTIONS FOR DISCUSSION

1. Should denominational publications be subsidized, or should they be priced so as to bring a margin of profit to the denomination?
2. What is the value of a weekly or monthly denominational paper?
3. Should the editor take sides on theological or political issues in his editorials, or should he remain neutral?
4. What is the value of having a neutral rather than a denominational incorporate name for a publishing house?
5. What contributions have foreign-language religious newspapers made to the national life of America?
6. Give arguments for and against a Christian newspaper or periodical carrying advertisements.
7. Give arguments for and against religious bookstores selling secular books.
8. Select one issue of a religious periodical and evaluate each article as to the benefits you derive from it.
9. Write a gospel tract. Indicate the type of reader you have in mind.
10. Select two tracts, one which you consider good, the other inferior. Give reasons for your evaluation.

15

Church-Sponsored General Education

STUDY OUTLINE

I. *A Dual System of Education.*

In the United States of America we have developed two parallel systems of education, the one sponsored by the state, the other by the church. This is thought by some to be unfortunate, by others to be desirable. There are leaders in the church who insist that since we have adopted an American policy of the separation of church and state in political matters, we should adhere to it in education as well. They hold that the state should provide general education through a system of secular public schools, and that the church should provide specialized Christian education within the church. There are, however, others who stress the fact that children are not dual personalities who may be administered to secularly by the state and spiritually by the church, but that they must be dealt with as integrated personalities. If religion is to become more than a Sunday response to a religious stimulus, it must become inter-

191

woven with the daily experiences of the child in the school as well
as in the church and home.

II. *The Church and Education.*

The church may wield its influence in general education in three
ways. First, it may establish its own system of education, sponsored
and paid for by the church. This is generally called the parochial
school system. In the second place, the church may encourage its
young people to prepare for teaching in the public schools. These
Christian teachers may thus wield a Christian influence, even
though religion is not taught as a formal subject. The Roman
Catholic Church makes use of both of these methods. Catholic
parochial schools are found in every diocese. Besides that, the
clergy encourages Catholic families to send their daughters, in
particular, to the Normal Colleges to prepare for public education.
Several of our larger city school systems are thus dominated by
Roman Catholic teachers and principals. The Roman Church
takes advantage of every legitimate opportunity at its disposal.
A third way of influencing general education is for Christian citizens to seek positions on the school boards and to become active in
Parent-Teacher Associations.

For more than a century the Roman Catholic church has conducted a nation-wide educational system of its own. In the school
year 1947–48 the Catholics of the United States maintained: 221
colleges and universities with an enrollment of 220,226; 338 seminaries and scholasticates with 23,701 students; 2,432 high schools
and academies with 506,397 students, and 8,248 elementary schools
with 2,274,840 pupils. The total number of American youth under
Catholic instruction was estimated at 4,138,695.[1] The goal of
Roman Catholicism is *every Catholic child in a Catholic school,* yet
it is estimated that only one-third of nominal Catholics are enrolled
in their parochial schools.

Among the Protestants, the Lutherans and the Seventh Day Adventists have been the leaders in parochial education. The former,
represented by four synods in 1949, had an enrollment of 110,282;
the latter had 33,540. Among the Protestant Episcopal Churches,
there are about seventy schools. Members of the Christian Reformed
church, though not a large denomination, have for a number of
years conducted parent-controlled private schools. In 1920 they
formed an organization, the *National Union of Christian Schools.*
In 1957 there were two hundred and seven elementary and secondary

---

[1] Philip Henry Lotz, *Orientation in Religious Education,* p. 519.

schools with a total enrollment of 40,754 that were members of this union. It is believed that about half of the children of Christian Reformed homes attend these schools.[2] The Mennonites have also established a number of parochial schools. In 1947 a new organization of interdenominational scope was organized as the *National Association of Christian Schools.* The 1957-58 *Annual* lists 141 schools as members, with an enrollment of 17,504.

III. *The State and Education.*

The constitution of the United States in its original form makes neither provision for, nor mention of, general education. It was the Tenth Amendment (1791) that indirectly delegated education to the state.

"The powers not delegated to the United States by the Constitution, nor prohibited by it to the States, are reserved to the States respectively, or to the people." This *Bill of Rights,* as it is commonly called, is broad enough in its scope to include education. The Ordinance of 1787 set up in the organization of Northwest Territory—which later became the states of Ohio, Indiana, Illinois, Michigan, and Wisconsin—refers to education, though no plan of action nor delegation of responsibility is presented. "Religion, morality, and knowledge being necessary to good government and the happiness of mankind, schools and the means of education shall forever be encouraged."

In early colonial times the church assumed responsibility for education. Sectarian rivalry, however, tended to make education a theological battlefield rather than a church-sponsored program of instruction. Horace Mann (1796–1859), as secretary of the Massachusetts State Board of Education, prepared painstaking annual reports that came to be circulated in neighboring states as well as in his own state. Later Henry Barnard (1811–1900) became secretary of the Connecticut Board of Education. These two men became leaders in the establishing of state control of education. Irish Catholics and German Lutherans fought together against the state-dominated movement. Mann was considered by many of the church leaders to be an enemy of Christianity, an agnostic, an atheist, an anti-Christ. In his Seventh Annual Report (published 1844) he recommended:

1. That religious teaching should be substituted for the dominant theological type, or, if people preferred to call the existing

2 Frank Gaebelein, *Christian Education in a Democracy,* p. 105.

instruction religious, it should be replaced by moral instruction and training.

2. That corporal punishment should be abolished.
3. That ample provision should be made for the training of teachers.
4. That oral methods should be used in preference to relying entirely upon textbooks.

These recommendations constitute an interesting commentary on the general educational practices of that day. Mann's attitude towards the church-sponsored education was misinterpreted. His criticism was not directed against the church nor against the religious content of education, but against the abuses that arose because of strong sectarianism. The educational controversy became involved in the theological disputes that were waged in New England between the liberal Unitarian faith and the conservative Protestants. The controversy came to center in Horace Mann because, in addition to being an advocate of new and dangerous educational doctrines, he was also a Unitarian. It was charged that he and his associates were responsible for the elimination from the school of the shorter catechism and direct religious and theological instruction.[3] Political parties inserted educational planks in their platforms. From New England the controversy spread westward until a battle line was formed in Wisconsin and Minnesota.

IV. *Controversies between Church and State.*

There were several settlements of Norwegian immigrants in Wisconsin in the 1860's. H. A. Preus, president of the Norwegian Lutheran Synod, in a visit to Norway in 1867, gave a series of lectures in which he sharply criticized the American public school system. He declared that he was unwilling to commit Norwegian Lutheran children to teachers who were Catholics, Methodists, or Atheists.[4]

Upon his return to America, President Preus continued his harangue against the "godless" schools of this country. He was heartily supported by a Norwegian Lutheran circuit rider, Bernt J. Muus. The controversy was carried into the Norwegian-American press. Two professors at Augsburg Seminary, Sven Oftedal and George Sverdrup, took issue with Preus and Muus. Oftedal argued that all Norwegian children in America should go to the public schools in order to become Americanized. Sverdrup declared his faith in the principle of the separation of church and state: "Let the

---

[3] Paul Monroe, *Founding of the American Public School System,* p. 263.
[4] Theodore C. Blegen, *Norwegian Migration to America,* p. 275.

school of religion be and continue to be the business of the congregation, and let the state continue to be without religious instruction as before."

The editor of *Skandinavien* carried the debate to the conference floor of the synod, hinting that the spurning of the American public school might well be considered an act of treason. Rasmus Sorensen, a Danish schoolmaster, in a lengthy article published in *Emigranten* warned that, if the counsel of the Norwegian clergy was followed, the children of the immigrants would become "Norwegian Indians in America."

In 1869 Muus came into heavy combat with a superintendent of public schools in Goodhue County in Minnesota. In reporting the annual educational events within his county, this superintendent stated that he had experienced hostility from the Scandinavian clergy who considered the public schools to be heathen institutions. Muus interpreted that comment to be directed against himself as well as the clergy of his synod. He responded in a polemic entitled *Schools and a Good School.* In this he charged the public schools with working against God.

Lutheran youth, he insisted, should be kept away from such dangerous influences. In the heat of the discussion he went so far as to ridicule the teaching of United States history in the public schools. The children of the native Indians, he insisted, were educationally better off than the white children who attended the public schools. Through the *Goodhue County Republican* the superintendent gave a spicy rebuttal. He referred to Muus as a "foreign priest and aristocrat who believes in perpetuity in America of a foreign language, a foreign continent, and foreign institutions." Debates of this type, whether waged in the press or from the speakers' platform, usually generate more heat than light and rarely result in any constructive measures.

At the synodical conference in 1873, President Preus presented an educational thesis that had been carefully prepared. These were the chief proposals:

1. To establish Norwegian-English congregational schools.
2. To bring about the appointment of Lutheran parochial teachers to the public schools.
3. The development of teacher-training at their Iowa School, Luther College.
4. The establishment of academies in Norwegian communities.
5. To secure the appointment of Lutheran teachers of the Norwegian language at American universities and colleges.

6. To give encouragement and help to Norwegian-American young people who wish to become teachers.

The thesis was printed and distributed, but no official action was taken regarding its suggestions, even though the thesis was presented at the synodical meeting the following year.

In 1874, the year of the second presentation of Preus' educational thesis, Muus announced the opening of an *evangelical Lutheran high school* at Northfield, Minnesota. The objective expressed was that of giving to confirmed youth a higher education for practical work than the home school could offer, and to direct the moral conduct of youth. On January 8, 1875, the school opened as a Christian academy. Later it developed into the well-known St. Olaf College. From their earlier controversy over parochial versus public schools, Preus and Muus turned their attention to Christian education on a secondary level.

V. *Christian Academies.*

The name *Academy* can be traced back to the park where the Greek philosopher Plato gave his instruction. This park was called *Academus* in honor of the owner of the land. The relationship of Plato's academy to that of the American academies was only in name.

During the persecution of the Puritans by the state church of England, the harsh *Act of Conformity* drove two thousand pastors from their parishes. The children of the dissenters were excluded from grammar schools and universities. The result was that these dissenters established schools for their own children, taught by teachers who were also dissenters.

John Milton (1608–1674), the English poet, in writing his now famous *Tractate on Education,* had proposed a new type of school to which he gave the name of the school of Plato, the Academy. This idea of the academy became the pattern for these dissenter schools which came to be called *Academies.* Milton believed that the entire education of a boy could be given in the academy without the division into secondary school and university. He held that "all this may be done between twelve and one and twenty, less time than is now bestowed in pure trifling at grammar and sophistry." Since Milton too was a nonconformist, it was but natural that his proposed pattern of education should greatly influence the curriculum and teaching methods of these nonconformist academies.

Benjamin Franklin founded the first academy in America in

1751, at Philadelphia.[5] The Academy movement spread throughout our country, and for a whole century served as the institution for secondary education. Our interest now is with the Christian or church-sponsored academy. In the efforts of the Protestant church to establish liberal-arts colleges throughout our nation, it has sometimes forgotten the contributions made by these Protestant secondary schools. As an educational agency in the frontier movement, they are second only to the church-sponsored college. In many instances these Christian academies became the people's colleges, for they gave a practical education on an adult level. The students were not the pleasure-loving, gay crowd of teenagers one often sees in the modern high school. They were serious-minded, knowledge-seeking, older young people and adults. Unmarried immigrant men enrolled for the winter season in order to study English. Most of these academies became boarding schools.

Some of these academies began as private ventures by ambitious clergymen. They began in the parsonage, continued in the church building, and finally acquired a campus and buildings of their own. The schools fortunate enough to be adopted by a synodical conference or some other aggregate of churches usually survived, while those which remained orphaned died in their infancy from malnutrition. The Protestant educational cemetery hides many such tragedies. That many of these now-dead academies entertained from their origin high hopes to grow into colleges is evidenced by their names: Minnesota College, Texas Wesleyan College, and Walden College.

Since educational standards of these schools were not set by any accrediting body, they tended to be quite flexible. Some classes were conducted on a college level, since the teachers were recent university graduates. Others were little more than a glorified elementary instruction. The courses taught, besides English, were usually United States History, Ancient and Medieval History, Mathematics, and Science. Such foreign languages as Latin, German, French, and Greek were offered. In the schools sponsored by Scandinavian churches, courses in the Scandinavian (Swedish, Norwegian, Danish) languages and culture played a very important part. Bookkeeping, typewriting, and penmanship constituted the commercial department. Courses in music were added. Many of the teachers were clergymen, some of them supplementing their

---

[5] This Franklin Academy in 1775 developed into a college which became the educational grandparent of the University of Pennsylvania.

meager salaries by serving some church. Courses in Bible were required of all students. The head of the Academy was called the president. Besides teaching, he was responsible for raising the funds for carrying on the work of the institution. David Brunstrom, president of Walden College, Kansas, upon retiring from office to become a pastor, reported that during the year just past he had taught six hours a day such varied subjects as Latin, English, literature, general history, geometry, Swedish, and Christianity, while on Sundays he had preached and on Mondays solicited funds for the school. The critical condition of the school can be appreciated when we learn that it was decided to discontinue the high-school department but continue the music and commercial courses. Teachers were to be paid on commission; in order to save expense, no new catalogs would be printed, and a man from a local church of another denomination was to lead the chapel services and serve as principal.[6] The school under such desperate circumstances could not survive. The campus was sold to the Free Methodists, who have succeeded in developing a liberal arts college.

Many of these academies came into being as additions to the frontier schools for the training of ministers and missionaries. These candidates for the ministry, though filled with spiritual zeal and fervor, were sadly lacking in general education. Because of the general nature of their ministry among the prairie pioneers and forest dwellers, the four years of college plus three years of formal theological training was out of question. Some of these candidates were in their late twenties and early thirties. Most of them had had no high school training, and a few had not even completed the elementary school. They did, however, have considerable talent in addition to their zeal. Shortened courses in training for this frontier ministry therefore became a necessity. In some of the smaller seminaries two teachers were engaged, one to teach Bible, the other to teach such subjects as English, history, science, and public speaking. These secular classes developed into a department commonly called the academy, that was preparatory to the training for the ministry. Theoretically the academy courses were to be taken before entering upon the theological training, but for practical reasons students were permitted to pursue studies in both areas simultaneously.

Young people, especially men, not planning for the ministry would enroll in the academy and be permitted to take some of the

---

6 Kansas *Missionstidning*, July, 1911, issue.

Bible courses. Gradually these academies became college preparatory in nature, and the curricula and length of school terms, require-
ments for graduation, and so forth, became standardized.

Since the close of the First World War these Christian academies have declined in number until at present they are almost ex-
tinct. There are several reasons for this decline. The greatest is,
no doubt, the competition with the public high schools. These are
tax-supported and thus are able to secure adequate buildings and
equipment. The public high school is able to offer a large variety
of courses which are beyond the range of the small academy, where
a fixed curriculum is for practical reasons a necessity. A second
reason is the transfer of church interest to higher education, as dispensed by liberal arts colleges. The tragedy seems to be that after
academies have developed into accredited four-year colleges, the
secondary education becomes delegated to the public high schools.
The biography of a large number of our Christian colleges is that
they were born as academies (on the secondary level), added college
courses year by year until they attained college stature, then continued to carry the academy as a sort of historical appendage sharing the same campus, until finally, for financial as well as for
college-expansion reasons, the academy was sloughed off.

That the heyday for the academy is a matter of past history is
evident. No longer do our seminaries need secondary schools to
supplement the theological training, since college training is now
a prerequisite for entrance. During the early part of our present
century, public high schools were not found in a large number of the
towns of the rural areas. The young people who wanted secondary
education had to go to the cities to live with relatives or friends of
the family. These Christian academies ministered to large numbers of rural youth. Now there are good public high schools where
youth may live at home while attending. If it is a choice between
living in a Christian home while attending a secular high school,
or attending a Christian school in a city away from home during
these formative years of early adolescence, one might be inclined
to favor the former. There is, nevertheless, still a need for Christian secondary schools. In situations where a child may live at home
while attending a Christian high school, much can be said in favor
of it. Many sincere Christian parents are concerned about the com-
panions and social life associated with the large urban high schools.

There are wealthy parents who for social reasons are anxious to
send their children to private schools. The religious interest is but
secondary. Christian academies may render a spiritual ministry to
such families. To some parents the academy is a glorified reform

school. Youngsters who tend to be incorrigible and do not get along in the public schools are sent to Christian schools in the hopes that they may be reformed.

The average American Protestant surrenders his child to the state for elementary education, but the growth of the public high school has crowded the church-sponsored academy almost out of the educational picture; not intentionally, but in reality nevertheless. The church of today, therefore, focuses largely on Christian *college* education. With the growth and expansion of state colleges and universities, there is a question how long the church can continue its higher education. It seems that the church is retreating step by step before the advance of the state. The problem is far more serious than the average American Protestant realizes. Roman Catholic leaders have long been alert to the situation and have gone to great pains to develop a Roman Catholic-controlled education.

The secularization of Protestant higher education has meant that, aside from a few highly diluted courses in Christianity (required but by no means popular) and weekly chapel services with some reference to religion, the program of the Christian colleges differs very little from that of the state college on the same academic level. The recent rise of a large number of Bible colleges and Fundamentalist universities should call to our attention that nothing but a traditional Christian college is meeting the need of our Protestant public.

VI. *The Christian College.*

These church-sponsored colleges have contributed much to the culture of our country as outposts of the westward-moving civilization. The story of the westward frontier is more than a parade of Indians and cowboys; it includes the circuit rider who dispensed the gospel as he traveled on foot or on horseback. It should also include the pioneer college professor and his colorful students.

The mortality of these pioneer colleges was high. It was not a matter of accidental death, but of economic starvation. The erecting of college buildings came to be conference competitive rather than denominationally planned. It is the erection of large buildings that has become the near ruin of many small colleges. When an institutional debt depresses the morale of the personnel, the work becomes inferior. Teachers who fail to draw enough salary to pay their own grocery bills can scarcely be expected to teach courses in economics in a calm, unbiased, and scholarly manner. When money solicited for educational purposes must be used to pay interest on old debts, it is difficult to arouse the public to an appreciation of the glory of higher education.

The Christian junior college has not achieved what was hoped for. One reason is that very few of the teachers and administrators have really understood the basic philosophy on which the junior college is based. The result has been one of two patterns, either that of an extended and glorified high school, or that of an undeveloped liberal-arts college with a feeling of academic inferiority. The other reason for the failure of the Christian junior college has been that, almost without exception, these colleges have not been satisfied with being junior colleges. Their ambition has been to grow up and become *senior* colleges, four-year, degree-granting institutions. Some have even dreamed of eventually becoming universities. They have failed to understand the real challenge of a Christian junior college.

The term Christian education has become a magic term. It represents something good, something highly desirable. We hear about it, we read about it, yet few seem to know exactly what it is, what makes education Christian. How can we identify it? How does it differ from other types of education? When is a school Christian?

The following standards have been suggested which may be applied to Christian education on all levels:

1. Christian objectives
2. Christian faculty
3. Christian sponsorship
4. Christian philosophy
5. Christian program
6. Christian atmosphere
7. Christian product

VII. *Problems of Church-Sponsored Education.*

   1. Competition with state-sponsored education
      a. Parochial schools vs. public elementary education
      b. Christian academies vs. public high schools
      c. Christian colleges vs. state universities
   2. Inadequate resources
      a. endowments
      b. donations
      c. denominational budgets
   3. Prestige of state universities
      a. athletic program
      b. degree recognition
   4. Limitation of courses offered by Christian schools
   5. Lack of support by the Christian church
   6. Limited facilities for advanced studies and research

7. Competition between church-sponsored schools
8. Secularization of Christian education

VIII. *The Future of Christian Colleges.*

We may predict the future by observing trends in the past and present. In 1904 George Albert Coe made an analysis of denominational colleges:

> The denominational college appears, in fact, to be losing the distinctive marks which in other days set it off from all else. It seems indeed to be losing its consciousness of having a specific religious function; it seems to be thinking of itself chiefly as an institution for education in the so-called general sense. So true is this that friends of religious education have felt it incumbent upon them to start an agitation for the teaching of the Bible in Christian colleges.[7]

Thus, half a century ago, one of the leaders in Christian education sensed the trend. Today many of the so-called Christian schools are Christian only in a superficial way, for there is very little religion aside from chapel services and a few so-called Christianity courses with a minimum of true Christian content.

It seems quite evident that, if the Christian college is to survive, it must cease to compete with state-supported institutions and develop curricula that shall be definitely Christian. As a special type of educational institution, it can survive; as a mere copier of, and competer with, state colleges and universities, it is doomed to die. If it is to survive, it must retain its academic respectability, include courses not offered in state colleges, and promote a definite and positive Christian atmosphere. Above all things it must truly be Christian in spirit and in purpose.

REVIEW QUESTIONS

1. How do church leaders differ in their opinions regarding the church and education?
2. In what three ways may the church wield an influence in education?
3. How many colleges and universities did the Roman Catholics in the United States sponsor in 1947–48?
4. What was the total enrollment?
5. How many high schools and academies?
6. What enrollment?

---

[7] *Education in Religion and Morals,* p. 332.

7. How many elementary schools?
8. What enrollment?
9. What is the goal of the Roman Catholic Church educationally?
10. What two groups have been educational leaders among the Protestants?
11. How many were in 1949 enrolled in four Lutheran Synods?
12. How many among the Adventists?
13. What other church group has been active in Protestant education?
14. What organization did they form in 1920?
15. What was the enrollment in their schools in 1949?
16. When was the *National Association of Christian Schools* founded?
17. How does the Tenth Amendment to our constitution effect education?
18. Who was Horace Mann?
19. Who was Henry Barnard?
20. How was Mann misinterpreted?
21. Who was Preus?
22. What controversy did he precipitate?
23. What were the final results?
24. What were the Christian academies?
25. What are the seven standards suggested for evaluating a Christian college?

QUESTIONS FOR DISCUSSION

1. What are the advantages of having a dual system of education?
2. Should parents who send their children to private schools be exempt from paying school tax to the state? Why or why not?
3. To what extent does the state control private education?
4. What is the distinction between private schools and church schools? Give examples of both.
5. Is the church justified in discontinuing its academies in favor of higher education? Give reasons for your answer.
6. Should the denomination exact a school tax from its members in the same manner as the state does?
7. What courses should be offered in a church-sponsored college that are not offered in a state-sponsored school?
8. How would you differentiate between the following: church-sponsored college, Christian college, denominational college?
9. What are the advantages and disadvantages of training our future Christian leaders at large universities rather than at small Christian colleges?

10. What are the differences in educational philosophy between a Christian junior college and a Christian liberal-arts, four-year college?

16

The Recruiting and Training of Christian Workers

STUDY OUTLINE

I. *The Church Needs Workers.*

It has been God's plan to carry on his work on earth through human agencies. In the biblical narrative angels have appeared at certain occasions primarily to make announcements. The ministry of the Christian church has been through human beings. Many changes have been brought about during the centuries in the organization of the church, but there has been no substitute for human workers.

Every true Christian should be active in the church, but according to the Apostle Paul, there are diversities of gifts (I Cor. 12:4–31). The church needs to discover where each gift fits into the mosaic of the local church ministry. Not only does the modern church suffer for lack of consecrated workers; it sometimes suffers because of misplaced talents, the foot that tries to serve as a hand, and the ear that attempts to function as an eye, to use Paul's analogy of the church of Christ as a body.

II. *The Church Must Recruit Workers.*

We believe that God calls his workers; it may be a direct divine call to the individual, but God may also mediate his call through the local church. At the annual meeting of the local church, the members having prayed for divine guidance, they select candidates and then resort to the democratic policy of balloting to determine who shall serve. It is much the same method as that employed by the eleven disciples at Jerusalem in filling the vacancy caused by the suicide of Judas Iscariot. The disciples selected two candidates from the one hundred and twenty brethren. Then they prayed and cast lots (Acts 1:15–26). Likewise the seven "deacons" who were ordained to distribute the material means of the Jerusalem church were selected by the members; they chose, they prayed, and they "laid their hands upon them" (Acts 6:1–6). God's will may be revealed in and through Christians. We grant that the voice of the people in general is not the voice of God; but when sincere Christians focus their prayerful thinking upon a common problem, we have every reason to believe that God can and will reveal his will.

The local church should not only recruit the workers for its own ministry; it has a responsibility to recruit for the Christian work at large. There are workers who render services to the entire denomination, but they are nevertheless recruited from the local church. It is a member from the local church "X" that becomes a missionary to Africa, and it may be a member from the local church "Y" that becomes a candidate for a pastorate in the homeland. Whatever the training for the task they later receive, it is as members of a local church that the workers are recruited. In proportion to its membership, the small church usually sends more of its young people into Christian (full time) work than does the large church. One reason may be that in the small church each one must bear his burden of responsibility if the work of the church is to carry on, whereas in the large church there is the temptation for many to play the part of spectators, and often critics, while others work.

The local church, whether it be large or small, must put forth conscious effort to recruit and develop leadership, not only for its

own needs, but for the wider field as well. Every church should
have a spiritual garden plot where leaders are being grown for the
glory of God and the good of humanity. These leadership-growing
areas might well be in the teenage organizations of the church. The
opportunities afforded by our public schools for discovering and
developing leadership, especially on the secondary level, should
challenge the church to capitalize on these resources and channel
them into the life of the church. There is no reason why youth
who are active in the extra-curricular activities of high school
should become but spectators in the program of the church. Agres-
sive youth has need of being given directives. This calls for wise
supervision and co-operation. There are times when youth needs
to be restrained, other times when it needs to be spurred. A potential leader may become a nuisance because of an inflated ego. He
may be very conscious of his talents, and become "cocky" and over-
bearing. Unless he can dominate, he will not co-operate. Other
potential leaders have their future usefulness seriously handicapped
because they have not been given adequate assistance in preparing
themselves for their task. They have tried and failed. The result
is frustration and the beginning of an inferiority complex. The
one who would help youth develop its leadership must sense when
to praise and when to criticize. There is weeding as well as watering
in a garden plot.

III. *Varieties of Christian Work.*

Unfortunately there has developed in modern minds the idea
that Christian service is to be found primarily in the pastorate or
as a missionary on the foreign field. We have come to use the term
full-time Christian service to apply almost exclusively to these ordained ministries. The truth is that every Christian is, or should be,
in full-time Christian work. The choir member who on Sunday
sings forth the gospel should on Monday live forth the same gospel.
The Sunday-school teacher who interprets the Word of God to the
class on Sunday morning should illustrate that lesson in daily living
throughout the week. We have come to classify church workers
as belonging to the clergy or to the laity. It is true that ordination
is for a definite type of Christian work. We must not depreciate the
meaning of ordination. But we would with Martin Luther acclaim
the priesthood of every true believer.

Besides the pastor, there is in every church a staff of workers.
Most of these workers render their services without remuneration.
There are the members of the church board, with its deacons, dea-
conesses, and trustees. There are the choir members who proclaim

the gospel in song, the ushers who meet and greet the people who come to worship. Sunday-school teachers serve without pay, as do youth organization counselors. The growing practice of setting aside these elected and appointed lay workers in a public Sunday service helps to call to the attention of the church in general the dignity of the lay ministry.

In the more professional fields of Christian work there are, besides pastors, evangelists, and missionaries, also ministers of music, directors of youth work, teachers in Christian colleges, seminaries, and missionary training schools. New areas of specialized work are being developed from time to time. Any attempt to list all types of Christian work would be well-nigh impossible.

IV. *Training the Workers.*

Untrained volunteer workers may render valuable service to the cause of Christ. Zeal without knowledge, however, may result in irreparable harm. We may learn through the trial and error method, but it is usually a costly process. When some member of our family is in need of medical attention, we consult a well-trained, experienced, and licensed doctor. The body is too important to be surrendered to anyone using the trial and error method. When we send our high-school graduates to college, we choose the school carefully. We are not concerned primarily with the campus and its classrooms and dormitories; we consider the personality and training of the teachers. Teachers in the elementary schools, even in the kindergarten, must not only be trained, but their ability to teach must be certified. Where did those who are to educate our children receive their education? The human mind is a delicate mechanism; we cannot afford to take chances in having it abused or misdirected. But when it is a matter of our children's immortal souls and their spiritual welfare, we surrender them to inexperienced workers within the church, with the false notion that whatever happens within the four walls of the church and as a part of the program of the church must be good. Though the building has been formally dedicated to God, there is no guarantee that the workers are qualified to the task of the teaching ministry.

Although there have been individuals and groups within the Christian church that have deprecated an educated ministry, the general feeling has been that the pastor and missionary need training in order to do effective Christian work. There have in all generations been outstanding personalities who with but a minimum of training have accomplished a maximum of good. These are, however, exceptions rather than the usual experience. Harvard, the oldest college in America, was founded for the purpose of training clergymen. The oft-quoted words of its charter have stood through the years as a beacon light: "Dreading to leave an illiterate ministry to our churches, when our present ministers shall lie in the dust."

The academic training of these frontier preachers and circuit riders was usually very limited. Many had not had the benefit of a high school, much less college training. Their "professional" training consisted of a short course in Bible study. The training institutions that prepared these workers were in reality Bible institutes. The teachers were, in many instances, refined and cultured men having earned advanced degrees. Some of them were Greek, Hebrew, or Latin scholars. The training they dispensed was not a protest against the schooling they themselves had been given, but rather a temporary solution to a pressing problem. Many of these ministerial candidates were poor and could not afford an expensive schooling. The frontier churches, too, were poor and could not afford to support the faculty necessary for giving a full theological training. Gradually, strictly academic courses were added to the curriculum. The prerequisite of a high-school education for entering the seminary became a general practice. Gradually the prerequisite was expanded to two years of college, and finally the theological seminaries became graduate schools.

The preparation for service in foreign missions varied. The medical missionary passed through the regular medical school; missionary nurses trained at hospitals. In addition, certain courses in Bible institutes or missionary training schools were required. The missionaries themselves requested a more thorough training for future candidates and set good examples by devoting much of their furloughs to further studies. Besides studies in the field of missions and the Bible, courses in psychology, sociology, and philosophy have been added to the missions curriculum. Practically all of the denominations have their own theological seminaries, and some have several.

The fact that Bible institutes and nondenominational missionary training schools flourish is evidence that they are meeting a need not met by the Christian colleges and the theological seminaries. The Christian college should, in addition to the required Christianity or Bible courses, offer electives in the field of Christian work that would be of benefit to lay workers in the local church. Such courses could have both academic respectability and religious content.

It is in the area of training lay workers for the local church that we encounter our greatest problem. Sending these workers to the denominational training schools for short courses has been tried but has not proved successful, since the number reached has been altogether too small. To meet this need, courses have been prepared to be administered locally. The International Council of Religious Education has developed an extensive program of such courses. Since 1930 the Evangelical Teacher Training Association has likewise prepared training courses. Several denominations have prepared their own.

These courses are administered in different ways. In some instances they are offered as Home Study Courses (correspondence). In others they are sponsored by a group of churches in a town or community (interdenominationally). In many congregations the training is given by the local church for teachers in service as well as for prospective teachers. One evening a week for ten weeks in the autumn, and a similar period in late winter, provides an ongoing training. Some churches prefer to have two sessions one evening each week and thus cover the required number of sessions in fewer weeks.

Originally these training courses were planned for Sunday school teachers and were called *Teacher Training Courses.* One course that was used for many years was Charles A. Oliver's *Preparation for Teaching.*[1] Oliver was a Presbyterian minister. His course consisted of five ten-lesson units, all in one compact book. They dealt with Old Testament, New Testament, the Sunday School, Child Psychology, and Methods of Teaching. To cover all five of these areas in fifty lessons meant a very superficial study, yet the course was very helpful. Recently there has been a trend towards calling such courses as these *Leadership Training Courses,* thus not limiting the scope to Sunday-school teaching. Besides these courses a large number of books dealing with the teaching ministry of the local church have been published.

The person best qualified to teach these courses in the local church is usually the pastor. Public elementary and high school teachers, members of the church, may render a real service through teaching certain professional units on methods, while the pastor devotes himself to giving the Bible and general-content courses.

V. *Placing the Trained Workers.*

Graduates of the theological seminary are usually placed by the

---

[1] Originally copyrighted in 1909; 358,000 copies printed in twelve years. The book was translated into Swedish by a Yale Divinity School student, G. F. Hedstrand, under the title, *Undervisning i Konsten att Undervisa.*

denomination. The local churches present their requests to bishops, superintendents, the theological seminary, or some other denominationally acknowledged agency. Missionary candidates are selected and assigned by the board of missions.

Placing the trained worker in the local church is a bit more difficult. When the congregation calls a pastor, it selects one who is already trained and who perhaps has had considerable experience in the pastorate. Likewise when the church calls a minister of music or a director of youth work it is usually an outsider who is contacted. The church may be able to shop around before it finds the person it thinks will meet its needs. But in securing Sunday school workers, youth counselors, and so forth, it is making use of home talents. There should be some service that every true Christian can render. But not everyone is qualified to sing in the choir, and because of personality peculiarities there are those who cannot teach a class or be a counselor for youth. Some otherwise fine Christian would be far more successful as a policeman with uniform and badge, directing traffic at the street corner near the church, than he would if he attempted to lead a discussion in a Sunday-morning Bible class.

There have been instances when a person with eccentric theology and peculiar personality insisted on being given a Sunday school class because he had earned a teacher-training diploma. If we call the courses offered *Leadership* Training rather than *Teacher* training, the field of service would be wider. Some churches handle the problem by issuing annual calls to their teachers. At the end of any year a teacher who has apparently failed in teaching can without emotional stress be shifted to some other field of service within the church. Church workers need to be carefully selected even after training, in order that they may be placed in the positions where they can render the greatest service.

VI. *The Challenge of Trained Christian Leadership.*

1. *A denominational problem.* In our study our primary concern has been Christian education in the local church. We must, however, view Christian education with bifocals. There must be a recognition of the wider horizon of the denomination as well as attention to the local church. Even within the most democratic of evangelical church groups there is an overhead organization with its leaders. Some denominations seem to be top heavy with administrative offices and officers, while others function with a minimum number of such leaders.

These leaders have emerged from local churches, but often without adequate preparation for the offices they are to fill. Popularity rather than preparation is often the major factor in recruitment for denominational leadership. There are, however, hopeful trends in the direction of screening candidates for election to such offices. With the enriched curricula in theological seminaries, future clergymen, who usually constitute denominational leadership, will have had training in other fields than homiletics, church history, and theology. The requirement, for graduation, of at least one basic course in Christian education is an example of this broadened base of training.

2. *A local church problem.* The local church is responsible not only for recruiting and training leaders for its own local work, but for the development of potential leaders for the denomination as well. Denominational loyalty begins in the local church. The foundations of theology are laid in the local Sunday school. The superstructure is added in the Christian college and the theological seminary. The screening of volunteers for positions of leadership in the local church is a difficult task. If it were a matter of hiring paid workers, it might be possible to be more selective. Some volunteers overestimate their own ability, while others underestimate their own talents. The one who is responsible for the selection of workers cannot, therefore, accept them on the basis of their own testimony. Whether the congregation is large or small, every member should be active, but that activity should be in keeping with the person's talent and training. The aims of the Sunday school as expressed many years ago by Charles Oliver are still valid:[2]

> Every pupil a Christian;
> Every Christian a worker;
> Every worker trained.

3. *A dream of the future.* There are two general types of daydreams: the one basks in the glory of the past, while the other anticipates the future. The first type of dreamer is in danger of erecting tombstones in place of milestones. The second type of dreamer is likewise in danger; he may be guilty of an impractical idealism. But if there is to be progress, we must use the past, not as a hitching post, but rather as a signboard. We get our sense of direction; we profit by the mistakes we have made. Progress means change, but not all change is for the better. There may be a change that spells retrogression and deterioration. The sapling changes as it grows; the wind-uprooted tree changes also, but it disintegrates.

---

[2] *Preparation for Teaching* (revised), p. 157.

In our dream of the future we do not anticipate a church so dominated by the teaching ministry that the pulpit becomes of minor importance and the entire program of the local church is tooled for teaching. Rather, we would visualize the future church as giving to the teaching ministry its rightful place, without crowding out or even cramping the other ministries of the church.

The church of our dreams will not resemble a beehive swarming with life on Sunday and a morgue the other six days of the week. The congregation will not be passively seated in comfortable pews watching a few paid and trained workers perform. It will distribute the teaching ministry throughout the week with a concentration on Sunday. Besides the pastor, there will be well-trained women workers devoting their time to the church's ministry in the parish. The curricula used will be of the best, but the teaching will not be limited to the printed lesson materials. Those responsible for the teaching will not only be trained, they will be motivated. Every member of the church will have an active part in its ongoing ministry; a select few will serve on the teaching staff.

The ideal future church will not consist of a large congregation meeting once or twice a week in a downtown structure, but rather a well-knit family of families reaching out to contact other families in a residential area. We will still need our downtown churches and our large congregations, but they do not represent our dream of an ideal church. The future church will be concerned with the individual, but it will give more attention than in the past to the importance of the family units in which these individuals live. It will continue to preach and teach the gospel: "Believe on the Lord Jesus, and thou shalt be saved." But it will not omit, as is so often done in quoting that Pauline passage, "thou and thy house," (Acts 16:31). Methods of ministering will be streamlined, but the gospel content of the message will remain. With Paul, workers in the field of Christian education may say, "a great door and effectual is opened unto me," and he adds, "and there are many adversaries" (I Cor. 16:9). We will not achieve through mere dreaming or wishful thinking; we must be aware of obstacles (adversaries) as well as open doors. Never in the history of Christianity have the doors of Christian education been as wide open as they are today. These open doors offer a real challenge to an effective Christian ministry. "Go ye therefore, and make disciples of all the nations, baptizing them into the name of the Father and of the Son and of the Holy Spirit: teaching them to observe all things whatsoever I commanded you: and lo, I am with you always, even unto the end of the world" (Matt. 28:19, 20).

Review Questions

1. What does Paul say about the gifts within the church?
2. How *could* God call His workers?
3. How *does* He usually call them?
4. What examples do we have from the book of Acts of human and divine co-operation in calling workers?
5. In proportion to membership, which contributes the most candidates for Christian work, the small or the large church?
6. What may be the reason?
7. How may a local church secure its future workers?
8. What do we usually mean by *full time* Christian service?
9. Why is this phrase not altogether correct?
10. What is the distinction between *clergy* and *laity?*
11. What was Luther's point of view?
12. What is the purpose of ordination?
13. What do some churches do to recognize lay workers?
14. Was the academic training of the frontier preachers and the circuit riders high or low?
15. Why?
16. What is meant by a *graduate* school?
17. What commonly considered *secular* courses are of great value to missionaries?
18. How could the Christian colleges contribute towards the training of a lay leadership in the church?
19. Who was Charles Oliver?
20. What areas were included in his course?
21. How would a *leadership* course differ from a *teacher-training* course?
22. When may a diploma from a teacher-training class precipitate a problem?
23. How might such a problem be solved?
24. In what way must the local church render a dual service in recruiting workers?
25. In what different ways may local lay leaders be trained for their task?

Questions For Discussion

1. Besides the candidate's own testimony, what evidence do we have that the candidate has really been called by God?
2. If a minister of the gospel fails in his ministry, is that an evidence that he was mistaken in his call?

3. How may high-school-age youth know whether or not they are called into some special type of ministry?
4. Should the function of a theological seminary be to give training to all who enroll, or should it attempt to screen the candidates and refuse to admit those who do not seem to have the necessary aptitudes?
5. When may a Christian worker have too much training?
6. At what age should potential church workers be recruited and trained?
7. How may the saying, "A little learning is a dangerous thing," apply to Christian workers?
8. What courses preparing lay workers could be introduced in the regular curriculum of a denominational college?
9. How would you proceed to *recruit* workers in your local church?
10. How would you proceed to *train* them?

Bibliography

Armentrout, J. S. *Administering the Vacation Church School.* Westminster, 1928.

Athearn, Walter. *Character Building in a Democracy.* Macmillan, 1924.

————. *The Minister and the Teacher.* Century, 1932.

Bailey, Albert E. *The Arts and Religion.* Macmillan, 1944.

————. *Christ and His Gospel in Recent Art.* Scribner, 1948.

Betts, George H. *How to Teach Religion.* Abingdon, 1924.

Betts and Hawthorne. *Method in Teaching Religion.* Abingdon, 1925.

Bower, W. C. *The Curriculum of Religious Education.* Scribner, 1925.

Bower and Hayward. *Protestantism Faces its Educational Task Together.* Nelson, 1949.

Brooks, Fowler D. *The Psychology of Adolescence.* Houghton, 1929.

Brown, Arlo A. *A History of Religious Education in Recent Times.* Abingdon, 1923.

Bushnell, Horace. *Christian Nurture (revised).* Yale University, 1947.

Caldwell, Irene Smith. *Our Concern Is Children.* Warner, 1948.

Carrier, Blanche. *How Shall I Learn to Teach Religion?* Harper, 1930.

————. *Christian Education for Family Life.* Harper, 1937.

Chamberlin, J. Gordon. *The Church and Its Young Adults.* Abingdon, 1943.

Chappell, E. B. *Evangelism in the Sunday School.* Methodist Church South, 1925.

Chave, Ernest J. *A Functional Approach to Religious Education.* University of Chicago, 1947.

Cole, Luella. *The Psychology of Adolescence.* Rinehart, 1947.

Cubberley, Ellwood. *The History of Education.* Houghton Mifflin, 1930.

Dale, Edgar. *Audio-Visual Methods in Teaching.* Dryden, 1946.

Drought, R. Alice. *A Camping Manual.* Barnes, 1943.

Eby and Arrowood. *The History and Philosophy of Education— Ancient and Medieval.* Prentice-Hall, 1942.

————. *The Development of Modern Education.* Prentice-Hall, 1942.

Gaebelein, Frank E. *Christian Education in a Democracy.* Oxford, 1951.

Gift, Foster U. *Week-Day Religious Education.* Lutheran, 1926.

Gorham, Donald. *Understanding Adults.* Judson, 1948.

Groves, Ernest. *Christianity and the Family.* Macmillan, 1942.

Harkness, Georgia. *Understanding the Christian Faith.* Abingdon, 1947.

Harner, Nevin C. *The Educational Work of the Church.* Abingdon, 1939.

————. *Youth in the Work of the Church.* Abingdon, 1942.

Havighurst and Taba. *Adolescent Character and Personality.* Wiley, 1949.

Hayward, P. R. and M. H. *The Home and Christian Living.* Westminster, 1931.

Heim, Ralph. *Leading a Sunday Church School.* Muhlenberg, 1950.

Homrighausen, E. G. *Choose Ye This Day.* Westminster, 1943.

Horne, H. H. *The Philosophy of Christian Education.* Revell, 1937.

Johnson and Yost. *Separation of Church and State.* Minnesota, 1948.

Jones, Mary Alice. *The Church and the Children.* Cokesbury, 1935.

————. *The Faith of Our Children.* Cokesbury, 1943.

Leach, William H. *Church Publicity.* Cokesbury, 1930.

Lebar, Lois. *Children in the Bible School.* Revell, 1952.

Lindhorst, Frank A. *The Minister Teaches Religion.* Abingdon, 1945.

Lotz, Philip Henry. *Current Weekday Religious Education.* Abingdon, 1925.

————. *Orientation in Religious Education.* Abingdon, 1950.

McKibben, Frank. *Christian Education through the Church.* Cokesbury, 1943.

Maus, Cynthia. *Christ in the Fine Arts.* Harper, 1938.

————. *The World's Great Madonnas.* Harper, 1947.

Maves and Cedarleaf. *Older People and the Church.* Abingdon, 1949.

Mayer, Herbert C. *Young People in Your Church.* Revell, 1953.

Monro, Paul. *The Founding of the American School System.* Macmillan, 1940.

Moon, Alleen. *The Christian Education of Older People.* Cokesbury, 1943.

Munro, Harry C. *The Pastor and Religious Education.* Abingdon, 1930.

Ownbey, Richard. *Evangelism in Christian Education.* Abingdon, 1941.

Pendry and Hartshorne. *Organizations for Youth.* McGraw-Hill, 1935.

Peters, Donald. *Let's Go Camping.* Brethren Press, 1945.

Price, J. M. *A Survey of Religious Education.* Ronald Press, 1940.

Richardson, Norman E. *The Christ of the Classroom.* Macmillan, 1932.

Rogers and Vieth. *Visual Aids in the Church.*

Shaver, Erwin L. *A Christian Attitude Towards the Press.* University of Chicago, 1925.

————. *The Weekday Church School.* Pilgrim Press, 1956.

Sherrill, Lewis J. *The Rise of Christian Education.* Macmillan, 1944.

————. *Family and Church.* Abingdon, 1937.

————. *Understanding Children.* Abingdon, 1939.

Shields, Elizabeth. *Music in the Religious Growth of Children.* Abingdon, 1943.

Smart, James D. *The Teaching Ministry of the Church.* Westminster, 1954.

Stafford, Hazel Straight. *The Vacation Religious Day School.* Abingdon, 1920.

Stafford, Thomas Albert. *Christian Symbolism in the Evangelical Churches.* Abingdon, 1942.

Stock, Harry Thomas. *Church Work with Young People.* Pilgrim Press, 1929.

Strang, Ruth. *An Introduction to Child Study.* Macmillan, 1951.

Ulich, Robert. *History of Educational Thought.* American Book, 1950.

————. *The Fundamentals of Democratic Education.* American Book, 1940.

Van Dusen, H. P. *God in Education.* Scribner, 1951.

Vieth, Paul H. *Objectives in Religious Education.* Harper, 1930.

————. *The Church and Christian Education.* Bethany, 1947.

————. *The Church School.* Christian Education Press, 1957.

Wahlstrom, Catherine Lee. *Add Life to Their Years.* National Council of Churches, 1953.

Wardle, Addie Grace. *History of the Sunday School Movement in the Methodist Episcopal Church.* Methodist, 1918.

Whitehouse, Elizabeth. *The Children We Teach.* Judson, 1950.
Wilds, Elmer H. *The Foundations of Modern Education.* Rinehart, 1942.

Index

DATE DUE